Anonymous

Masonic Code of the Grand Lodge of Utah. 1879

Containing the constitution and laws of the jurisdiction, ancient charges,

blank forms, &c

Anonymous

Masonic Code of the Grand Lodge of Utah. 1879
Containing the constitution and laws of the jurisdiction, ancient charges, blank forms, &c

ISBN/EAN: 9783337219703

Printed in Europe, USA, Canada, Australia, Japan

Cover: Foto ©Suzi / pixelio.de

More available books at **www.hansebooks.com**

PREFACE.

GRAND LODGE OF UTAH, ANCIENT, FREE AND ACCEPTED MASONS.
OFFICE OF THE GRAND SECRETARY,

SALT LAKE CITY, March 22d, 1879.

THIS WORK is designed for the use, and to meet the wants and demands of the Masonic Fraternity in this Grand Jurisdiction. It embraces the Constitution and Laws of the Grand Lodge, Ancient Charges and Landmarks, Form of Record for Lodges and Trial Record and all necessary Blank Forms used by Lodges. It is published in pursuance of the authority given by the Grand Lodge at its Seventh Annual Communication, November 12th and 13th, A. D. 1878, and after having been examined and approved by the M∴ W∴ Grand Master, Thomas Edward Clohecy, is fraternally dedicated to the Craft in Utah.

Christopher Diehl
Grand Sec'y.

General Index.

CONSTITUTION

OF THE

MOST WORSHIPFUL GRAND LODGE

OF

ANCIENT, FREE AND ACCEPTED MASONS OF UTAH.

———

WHEREAS, Each Grand Lodge possesses the inherent power to form a Constitution, as the Fundamental Law of its Masonic actions, and to enact such By-Laws, from time to time, as it may deem necessary for its own government, and to make such Rules and Regulations for the administration of its constituent Lodges, as will insure the prosperity thereof, and promote the general good of Masonry; and

WHEREAS, Each Grand Lodge is the true representative of all the Fraternity in communication therewith, and is in that behalf an absolute and independent Body, with supreme legislative authority, provided always that the Ancient Landmarks of Freemasonry be held inviolate;

Therefore, Upon these principles, which have never been disputed, the Grand Lodge of Ancient, Free and Accepted Masons of Utah does hereby ordain, establish and promulgate the following Constitution for its future government, and does make and prescribe the following Rules and Regulations for the government of the Lodges under its jurisdiction.

ARTICLE I.

Grand Lodge--Title of.

This Grand Lodge shall be entitled, "The Most Worshipful Grand Lodge of Ancient, Free and Accepted Masons of Utah."

———

ARTICLE II.

Jurisdiction of.

This Grand Lodge is the only source of authority and exercises exclusive jurisdiction in all matters pertaining to Ancient Craft Masonry in the Territory of Utah.

ARTICLE III.

Rank and Title of Officers and Representation in—Proxies.

The Grand Lodge shall consist of a Grand Master (whose address shall be Most Worshipful), a Deputy Grand Master, a Senior Grand Warden, a Junior Grand Warden, a Grand Treasurer and a Grand Secretary (whose addresses shall severally be Right Worshipful), a Grand Chaplain, a Grand Orator, a Grand Lecturer, a Grand Marshal, a Grand Standard Bearer, a Grand Sword Bearer, a Senior Grand Deacon, a Junior Grand Deacon, a Senior Grand Steward, a Junior Grand Steward and a Grand Tyler (whose addresses shall severally be *Worshipful*), and such other Grand Officers as the Grand Lodge, from time to time, may appoint, and also Past Grand Masters, Past Deputy Grand Masters, Past Grand Wardens, Past Grand Treasurers and Past Grand Secretaries; together with all Past Masters of Lodges in this jurisdiction, the Worshipful Masters and Wardens, for the time being of the several chartered and duly constituted Lodges under the jurisdiction of this Grand Lodge, or their legally appointed Proxies, *provided*, such Representative or Proxy be a Master Mason and a member of the Lodge he represents, and produces a letter of Proxy, together with the resolution of his Lodge, under its seal, authorizing the appointment of such Proxy.

ARTICLE IV.

Annual Communication and Proceedings for Call of Special Communications of.

The Grand Lodge shall hold a regular Communication at least once in each year, at such time and place as may be designated in its By-Laws; but Special Communications may be ordered by the Grand Master (or in his absence from the Territory, or inability to attend, by the Deputy Grand Master, or the other presiding officer for the time being), whenever in his opinion the welfare of the Fraternity shall require it, and every such order for a Special Communication shall state the object thereof, so far as it is proper to be written, and each constituent Lodge under this jurisdiction shall have thirty days notice of such Communication, and no business shall be transacted thereat, except such as is specified in said order.

ARTICLE V.

Quorum, When Grand Lodge may be Opened.

The Grand Lodge shall not be opened, nor shall any business be transacted therein, unless a majority of the chartered Lodges under its jurisdiction be represented, but a smaller number may meet and adjourn from day to day, until the above provided representation shall attend.

ARTICLE VI.

Who Eligible to Office in Grand Lodge—Grand Masters &c. must be Past Masters of this Jurisdiction.

No Brother shall be eligible to office in this Grand Lodge who is not at the time of election or appointment a member, in good and regular standing, of a Chartered Lodge constituent to this Grand Lodge, and no Brother shall be eligible to the office of Grand Master or Deputy Grand Master, who is not a Past Master, having been duly elected and having presided over a Lodge under the jurisdiction of this Grand Lodge.

ARTICLE VII.

Number of Votes Prescribed.

SECTION 1. Each of the Grand officers for the time being, except the Grand Tyler, and each elective Past Grand Officer, when present at the meeting of the Grand Lodge shall be entitled to a vote; each Lodge shall be entitled to three votes by its proper officers, or, in their absence, their Representatives, and Past Masters not otherwise entitled to vote shall be entitled, collectively, to one vote.

How Lodges shall Vote in Grand Lodge.

SEC. 2. In case a constituent Lodge has but one Representative present, he may cast three votes; if two Representatives be present, the highest in rank shall cast two votes, and the lowest, one, if three Representatives be present, they shall cast but one vote each.

ARTICLE VIII.

Election and Appointment of Grand Officers.

. At each Annual Communication there shall be elected, on the second day by ballot: a Grand Master, a Deputy Grand Master, a Senior Grand Warden, a Junior Grand Warden, a Grand Treasurer and a Grand Secretary.

All other Grand officers shall be appointed by the Grand Master elect, but no Grand Officer shall assume the duties of his office until he shall have been duly installed. A majority of all the votes cast shall be necessary for an election.

ARTICLE IX.

Powers and Authority of the Grand Lodge.

SECTION 1. This Grand Lodge may grant Dispensations and Charters for holding regular Lodges of Free and Accepted Masons in Utah, and in other Territory, where no Grand Lodge exists, with the right to confer therein the several degrees of Entered Apprentice, Fellow Craft and Master Mason, and when deemed expedient and for good cause, may annul, revoke or amend such Dispensation or Charter, or any pre-existing Dispensation or Charter.

2

Its Legislative, Administrative and Appellate Jurisdiction.

SEC. 2. This Grand Lodge has original and exclusive jurisdiction over all subjects of Masonic legislation and administration, appellate jurisdiction and administrative jurisdiction from the decisions of Worshipful Masters, and from the decisions and acts of Lodges, and when expedient, has original jurisdiction over its Officers, members and Worshipful Masters, and its enactments and decisions upon all questions shall be the supreme Masonic Law of the Territory.

To Fix Geographical Limits of Lodges.

SEC. 3. This Grand Lodge may assign the limits and fix the location of each Lodge under its jurisdiction, and settle all controversies that may arise between different Lodges, and has the final decision and determination of all matters of controversies or grievances which may be brought up by appeal or otherwise.

To Make Laws for Lodges.

SEC. 4. It may make and adopt general Laws and Regulations for the government of the several Lodges under its jurisdiction, and at pleasure may alter, amend or repeal the same.

To Collect Dues from Lodges.

SEC. 5. It may assess and collect from the several Lodges under its jurisdiction such sums of money annually as may be provided for by Law and found necessary for the support and maintenance of the Grand Lodge.

To Supervise Finances.

SEC. 6. It may supervise the state and condition of its own finances, and adopt such measures in relation thereto as may be deemed necessary.

To Punish Members.

SEC. 7. It may reprimand, suspend or expel any member from its own Body for a violation of the Constitution, By-Laws and Regulations of the Grand Lodge, or for any other un-Masonic conduct; and may suspend or expel any accused person upon trial by appeal.

To Review the Doings of Grand Officers.

SEC. 8. This Grand Lodge shall at each Annual Communication consider and review the reports and doings of its Grand Officers for the past year, as well as those of the several Lodges under its jurisdiction. And finally may do whatsoever may be considered necessary to the well-being and prosperity of Ancient Craft Masonry.

ARTICLE X.

Powers, Prerogatives and Duties of Grand Master.

SECTION 1. The Grand Master has the power: 1st. To grant Dispensations for the formation of new Lodges under the Regulations provided herein and in the

By-Laws of this Grand Lodge. 2nd. To convene the Grand Lodge in special Communication for specified purposes. 3d. To preside at all special and regular Communications. 4th. To exercise the executive functions of the Grand Lodge when not in session. 5th. To decide all questions of usage, order and Masonic Law. 6th. To convene any Lodge within this jurisdiction, and in person, or by deputy, to preside therein, inspect their proceedings and require their conformity to Masonic rules. 7th. To suspend the functions of any Lodge for good reason. 8th. In person or by deputy to constitute Lodges, dedicate Masonic halls, lay corner-stones of Masonic halls, public buildings and structures. 9th. To appoint Representatives, by warrant, in any other recognized Grand Lodge and receive and accredit such Representatives from other Grand Lodges. 10th. To see that the Ancient Landmarks and Charges are observed, and to do and perform the duties of Ancient Grand Masters agreeably to the requirements of Masonry and this Grand Lodge.

Successor of Grand Master.

SEC. 2. In case of the death, absence or inability of the Grand Master, or a vacancy in his office, the Deputy Grand Master, Senior Grand Warden and Junior Grand Warden shall, in succession, succeed to his prerogatives and duties for all purposes.

Grand Treasurer—Duties of.

SEC. 3. It shall be the duty of the Grand Treasurer to take charge of all the funds and property of the Grand Lodge, to pay out no money except upon order of the Grand Lodge certified by the Grand Secretary, to report annually the amount of receipts and expenditures, by items, and from whom received and to whom paid and the amount of funds and property in his hands; and to execute and file with the Grand Secretary an official bond payable to the Grand Master or his successor in office, with sufficient sureties, to be approved by, and in such penalty as may be fixed from time to time, by the Grand Lodge, conditioned that he will pay or deliver, on demand, to the Grand Lodge, or to his successor in office, or properly account for all funds and property of the Grand Lodge, that shall come to his hands as Grand Treasurer.

Grand Secretary—Duties of.

SEC. 4. It shall be the duty of the Grand Secretary to record the transactions of the Grand Lodge; to receive, duly file and safely keep all papers and documents of the Grand Lodge; to prepare, sign and certify all Charters, Dispensations and other instruments from the Grand Lodge, and when necessary affix the seal of the Grand Lodge thereto; to receive and keep a proper account of all moneys of the Grand Lodge and pay over the same to the Grand Treasurer; to report annually to the Grand Lodge the amount of money received by him, by items, and the specific sources from which it was received; also the Lodges that have neglected to render proper returns and are in arrears, and such general information as to the state of the Lodges as may be proper for the information or action of the Grand Lodge; to conduct the correspondence of the Grand Lodge and to attend, with all necessary books and papers under his control, on all meetings of the Grand Lodge.

Grand Secretary—Compensation for Services.

SEC. 5. The Grand Secretary shall receive such compensation for his services as the Grand Lodge may direct, and in addition thereto shall receive the following fees, viz: 1st. For a dispensation to open a new Lodge, the sum of fifteen dollars. 2d. For a charter to perpetuate a Lodge, the sum of ten dollars. 3d. For a Dispensation to hold an election of an officer or officers, at another than the regular period, the sum of five dollars. 4th. For every certificate (except those hereinbefore named), requiring the seal of the Grand Lodge, the sum of two dollars.

ARTICLE XI.

Revenues—How Derived.

SECTION 1. The revenue of this Grand Lodge shall be derived from the following sources: 1st. For a Dispensation to form a new Lodge, the sum of fifty dollars. 2d. For a Charter to perpetuate a new Lodge, the sum of fifty dollars. 3d. For a Dispensation to hold an election of an Officer or Officers, at a time other than that hereinafter provided, the sum of ten dollars.

Grand Lodge Dues to be Paid by Lodges.

SEC. 2. The following contributions shall be paid as annual dues by each Lodge, whether chartered or under dispensation; 1st. For each degree it shall confer during the year, one dollar. 2d. For each Master Mason reported a member of a constituent Lodge in its annual returns (except such as are reported exempt from dues), the sum of three dollars.

Assessments may be Levied.

SEC. 3. The Grand Lodge may levy upon the constituent Lodges, subject to its jurisdiction, such contributions as may be required to defray proper expenses, which shall always be equal and uniform in proportion to the membership of the Lodges.

Other Revenues of Grand Lodge.

SEC. 4. Any sums realized out of the property of dissolved Lodges.

ARTICLE XII.

Lodges U. D.—How a Dispensation may be Obtained. Skill of New Master.

SECTION 1. No Letter of Dispensation shall be granted for the formation of a new Lodge, but upon the petition of seven known and approved Master Masons,

in which their first Master and Wardens shall be nominated, which petition shall be accompanied by a recommendation from the Lodge nearest to the place in which the new Lodge is to be holden, and before any particular Lodge shall recommend any petition for a new Lodge, they shall require the Brother named as Master, or one of the Brothers named as Wardens, to appear in open Lodge and be examined as to his proficiency in the work of the three degrees in Masonry, to the satisfaction of the Lodge.

Duties of Lodges Recommending Petition for Dispensation.

SEC. 2. Any constituent Lodge recommending a petition for a new Lodge, shall state explicitly that the Brethren whose petition she recommends have provided a suitable and safe Lodge room, and that the Master, or at least one of the Wardens of the proposed new Lodge, has appeared in open Lodge and been examined in the work of the three degrees in Masonry, and passed such examination in a creditable manner.

Application for Charter—Dispensation to be Returned—The Three Degrees must have been Conferred.

SEC. 3. Each Lodge under Dispensation shall return its Letter of Dispensation to the next Annual Communication after the date of said Letter, together with its record and other books and its petition for a charter, if desired, but no charter shall be granted to any such Lodge, unless it shall have conferred the degrees of Entered Apprentice, Fellow Craft and Master Mason.

ARTICLE XIII.

Powers and Duties of Constituent Lodges.

SECTION 1. The powers and duties of a Lodge are such as are prescribed in its Dispensation or Charter, by the Constitution, Laws and Regulations of this Grand Lodge, and the ancient usages of Masonry, and By-Laws, adopted by the Lodge for its own government, properly approved.

Constituent Lodges—When to Elect and Install Officers—Master must have been a Warden.

SEC. 2. Each constituent Lodge shall elect its Officers annually by ballot, by a majority of the votes of its members present, at the stated meeting next preceding the anniversary of St. John, the Evangelist; and they shall be installed on the evening of their election, or at such a time as then ordered by the Lodge, and they shall retain their respective offices until their successors in office shall be elected and duly installed. But no member shall be eligible to the office of Master who shall not have been duly elected and served as a Warden.

Meetings of Lodges.

SEC. 3. Each Lodge shall hold one, and may hold two regular meetings in each month, at which all business of the Lodge shall be transacted; but may hold such special meetings as it may determine or the Master order.

By-Laws of Lodges—Must be Approved by Grand Lodge.

SEC. 4. Each constituent Lodge shall have the right to adopt By-Laws for its own government, but no such By-Laws, nor any amendments thereto, shall be deemed valid until approved by the Grand Lodge. They shall be submitted for the approval of the Grand Lodge at its regular Communication next after their adoption, but they may be acted under, until such Communication, if approved by the Grand Master.

Must have a Seal, and file Impression with Grand Secretary.

SEC. 5. Each constituent Lodge shall procure a seal and file an impression of the same in the Grand Secretary's office to be carefully preserved.

Representation, Returns and Dues of Lodges to Grand Lodge.

SEC. 6. Each Lodge shall be represented in every Annual Communication of the Grand Lodge, when it shall also furnish a correct account of its proceedings during the past year, in a form to be prescribed by the Grand Lodge, and make payment of its regular dues; and in case of the non-performance of these duties for two regular Communications, its charter may be declared forfeited.

Applicants must reside twelve Months in Utah. Rejected Petition Excluded for six Months.

SEC. 7. No Lodge in this jurisdiction shall receive an application for the degrees in Masonry, unless the applicant shall have been a resident within the jurisdiction during twelve months; and not of an applicant who has been rejected, within a less period than six months after such rejection.

No Credit for the Degrees.

SEC. 8. No Lodge in this jurisdiction shall confer any degree in Masonry upon credit.

Duties of Investigating Committees How and when to Dispose of Petitions.

SEC. 9. No Lodge shall ballot upon an application for the degrees in Masonry until it shall have been referred to a committee, whose duty it shall be to make strict examination into the moral and physical qualifications of the applicant. All applications for initiation or affiliation shall be made in writing, at a regular meeting of the Lodge, but shall not be acted upon until after the expiration of four weeks after its presentation

Only one Ballot for the three Degrees.

SEC. 10. No Lodge shall have more than one ballot for the three degrees, unless otherwise ordered by the Master.

Examination must be had in Open Lodge. Proficiency Necessary.

SEC. 11. No Lodge shall advance an Entered Apprentice or Fellow Craft to a higher degree, until upon strict examination in open Lodge he is found entirely proficient in the preceding degree.

Fees for the Degrees.

SEC. 12. No Lodge within this jurisdiction shall confer the three degrees for a less sum than seventy-five dollars.

Limit to Number of Degrees at one time.

SEC. 13. No Lodge shall confer degrees upon more than five candidates at any one meeting; nor shall confer more than one degree upon any one candidate at any one meeting, nor shall confer either of the degrees upon more than one candidate at a time.

Dimit to accompany Petition.

SEC. 14. No Lodge shall receive an application for affiliation unless it be accompanied by a proper dimit from the Lodge of which the applicant was last a member.*

Right of Appeal.

SEC. 15. In all cases of suspension or expulsion by a constituent Lodge, the Brother suspended or expelled may appeal to the Grand Lodge.

The Master rules his Lodge—He is amenable only to Grand Lodge.

SEC. 16. No appeal from any decision of the Master of a Lodge shall be taken to the body of the Lodge, nor shall any charge be entertained against him by his Lodge during his term of office, but he shall be amenable for his conduct to the Grand Lodge only.

Advancement can be had only in the Lodge in which previous Degree was received.

SEC. 17. No Entered Apprentice or Fellow-Craft shall be advanced to a superior degree in any Lodge except that in which he received the previous degree, unless by the consent, in writing, of that Lodge.

Notification to Grand Secretary of all Rejections, Expulsions, &c.

SEC. 18. In all cases where members of a Lodge are expelled or suspended, and when any applicant for initiation is rejected, the Secretary of such Lodge shall forthwith notify the Grand Secretary, who shall report all such actions quarterly, to all the Lodges.

----

*Standing Resolution.

Resolved, That any Master Mason, residing in Utah, and hailing from a Grand jurisdiction where no dimits are issued to members, may petition any Lodge in this Grand jurisdiction for affiliation without an accompanying dimit, providing he produces other satisfactory evidence that he is a Master Mason in good standing. (Adopted Nov. 12th, 1878.)

ARTICLE XIV.

How Lodges may be dissolved.

SECTION 1.   A Lodge may be dissolved: 1st. By a voluntary surrender of its charter, when such surrender shall have been accepted by the Grand Lodge; and 2d. By revocation of its charter by the Grand Lodge.

How to Surrender Charter.

SEC. 2.   The charter of a Lodge may be surrendered, if notice shall be given at a regular meeting that a resolution to that effect will be presented at the next succeeding meeting, and if at that meeting there shall not be seven members present who oppose such resolution; but no such act of surrender shall be considered final, until it shall have been approved by the Grand Lodge.

Forfeiture of Charter.

SEC. 3.   The charter of a Lodge may be forfeited: 1st. By disobedience of any provision of the Constitution or Regulations of the Grand Lodge; 2d. By disregard of the lawful authority of the Grand Master; 3d. By violation or neglect of the Ancient recognized usages of the Craft, or, 4th. By failure to meet during a period of six successive months.

No Charter can be Forfeited unless Charges are Presented and Investigated.

SEC. 4   But no charter shall be forfeited unless charges against the Lodge shall have been presented to and investigated in the Grand Lodge, of which charges the Lodge accused shall have had due notice, though the same may be arrested until the next Annual Communication, either by the Grand Lodge or the Grand Master, upon satisfactory reasons therefor being shown.

Forfeiture, etc., of Charter involves the Suspension of Members.

SEC. 5.   The forfeiture or arrest of the Charter of a Lodge involves the suspension of all its members from the rights and privileges of Masonry, excepting those who may be especially exempted from such effect.

Property of Lodges when Charter Declared surrendered or forfeited become. Property of Grand Lodge.

SEC. 6.   The surrender or forfeiture of the Charter of a Lodge, when declared by the Grand Lodge, shall be conclusive upon the Lodge and its members, and all its funds, jewels, furniture, dues and property of every kind, shall be the property of the Grand Lodge.

ARTICLE XV.

Miscellaneous—Arraignment of Masters.

SECTION 1.   Charges may be preferred against the Master of a Lodge for his power, violation of the Constitution or Regulations, or for un-Masonic con-

duct of any kind, by any three Master Masons in good standing; which charges shall be in writing over their signatures, and shall be presented to the Grand Lodge, if in session, or to the Grand Master during vacation; which charges shall be tried and determined in the manner prescribed by this Grand Lodge.

Standard Work to be Practiced by Lodges.

SEC. 2. This Grand Lodge shall adopt a standard of work and lectures, and each constituent Lodge shall practice the same, as adopted, and in case of willful violation of this provision by any such constituent Lodge, its Charter may be forfeited at the pleasure of the Grand Lodge.

The Ancient Constitution, the Fundamental Law.

SEC. 3. The Book of Constitutions, hereunto attached, this Grand Lodge does recognize and adopt as the fundamental Laws, Rules and Regulations for the government of Masons, and declares that it should be frequently read and perused by Masters and other Craftsmen, as well within the constituent Lodges as thereout to the end, that none may be ignorant of the excellent principles and precepts it inculcates.

Other Rules etc, may be Adopted.

SEC. 4. It shall be competent for the Grand Lodge to adopt such other Rules and Regulations as it may deem necessary, not inconsistent with this Constitution and the ancient Rules and Regulations of Freemasonry.

ARTICLE XVI.

Amendments—Must lay over one Year—Two-Thirds Vote by Lodges necessary.

SECTION 1. No amendments to this Constitution shall be made, unless the same, after being proposed in writing, shall be concurred in by a majority of the members present, and shall have been postponed for consideration until the succeeding Annual Communication, and if at that time it shall be adopted by a vote of two-thirds of the Lodges represented therein, the same shall become a part of this Constitution.

Amendments to By-Laws etc.—When to act upon—Two-thirds Vote.

SEC. 2. The By-Laws, Regulations, Edicts, Rules of Order, Trial Code and Standing Resolutions of this Grand Lodge may be repealed, altered or amended, at any regular Communication, by a vote of two-thirds of the members present.

BY-LAWS

MOST WORSHIPFUL GRAND LODGE

OF

ANCIENT, FREE AND ACCEPTED MASONS OF UTAH.

GRAND LODGE.

Annual Communication.

SECTION 1. The Annual Communication of this Grand Lodge shall be held at Salt Lake City, on the second Tuesday of November in each year.

Seal.

SEC. 2. It shall have a Seal, bearing such devices and inscriptions as may hereafter be determined, which shall be affixed to all instruments issued by or under its authority.

GRAND MASTER.

Annual Address—What it shall contain.

SEC. 3. The Grand Master shall, at the opening of each Annual Communication, submit a *written* address, setting forth an account of his official acts during the recess of the Grand Lodge, and such suggestions and propositions as he deems valuable to the Fraternity, and proper for the consideration of the Grand Lodge, and shall present with it his financial report.

To Exemplify the Work.

SEC. 4. The Grand Master shall cause the work and lectures on the three degrees in Masonry to be exhibited before the Grand Lodge at each Annual Communication.

To appoint Committees—Regular.

SEC. 5. The following regular Committees, to consist of three members each, shall be appointed by the Grand Master at each Annual Communication, as soon as practicable after its opening, viz: On Credentials, On Grand Master's Address,

SECTION 5. The following regular Committees, to consist of three members each, shall be appointed by the Grand Master at each Annual Communication, as soon as practicable after its opening, viz : On Credentials, On Grand Master's Address, On Grievance and Appeals, On Finance, On Lodges under Dispensation, On Returns, On Unfinished Business, the duties of which Committees shall cease at the close of such Communication. (Masonic Code, page 14.)

SECTION 6. The following Standing Committees shall also be appointed by the Grand Master at each Annual Communication, just before its close, viz: On Jurisprudence, to consist of five members, On Correspondence, On Library, and On the Standard Work, to consist of three members each, the duties of which Committees shall continue during the year thereafter, and shall cease at the close of the next succeeding Annual Communication. (Masonic Code, page 15.)

On Grievance and Appeals, On Finance, On Grand Lodge Library, On Lodges under Dispensation, On Returns, and, On Unfinished Business, the duties of which Committees shall cease at the close of such Communication.

Committees—Standing.

Sec. 6. The following standing Committees shall also be appointed by the Grand Master at each Annual Communication, just before its close, viz: On Jurisprudence, to consist of five members, On Correspondence, and, On the Standard Work, to consist of three members each, the duties of which Committees shall continue during the year thereafter, and shall cease at the close of the next succeeding Annual Communication.

Committees—Special.

Sec. 7. Special Committees may also be appointed by the Grand Master, whenever it may be deemed necessary by the Grand Lodge.

GRAND SECRETARY.

To Transmit Printed Proceedings.

Sec. 8. The Grand Secretary shall transmit three copies of the printed Proceedings of each Annual Communication to each Grand Lodge recognized by this Grand Lodge, three copies to each constituent Lodge in the jurisdiction, and one copy to each elective Grand Officer and elective Past Grand Officer.

To Print List of Suspensions, &c.

Sec. 9. The Grand Secretary, when publishing the Proceedings of this Grand Lodge, shall cause to be published therewith a list of all suspensions and expulsions under this jurisdiction.

To employ Assistant.

Sec. 10. The Grand Secretary may, with the approval of the Grand Master, appoint an assistant Grand Secretary, for whose official acts he shall be responsible, and who shall receive such compensation for his services as the Grand Lodge may, from time to time, direct.

To be Grand Librarian.

Sec. 11. The Grand Secretary (by virtue of his office), is hereby constituted Grand Librarian, and directed to take charge of the Grand Lodge Library, subject to such regulations as the Grand Lodge shall prescribe.

CONSTITUENT LODGES.

Annual Returns—What they shall Contain.

Sec. 12. Each Lodge under the jurisdiction of this Grand Lodge, shall, at least thirty days before each Annual Communication, transmit to the Grand Secretary the Annual returns of said Lodge, for the year ending, thirty days prior to such Annual Communication, in such form as the Grand Secretary shall provide, which shall embrace a list of Officers and members,* of initiations, passings, raisings, admissions, dimissions, rejections, suspensions and expulsions, restorations and deaths, with their respective dates, which return shall be signed by the Master and Secretary, and attested under the seal of the Lodge, and with such annual return shall pay to the Grand Secretary all sums due from such Lodge to the Grand Lodge.

Returns and Dues entitle to Representation.

SEC. 13. No Lodge shall be entitled to a representation in this Grand Lodge, unless the returns have been made and dues paid as prescribed in the previous section.

Material Jurisdiction of Lodges.

SEC. 14. No Lodge shall receive and act upon the petition of an applicant for initiation whose residence may be nearer some other Lodge under this jurisdiction than the one to which application is made, without the consent of such nearest Lodge.

Unanimous Consent for Withdrawal of Petition.

SEC. 15. No petition shall be withdrawn after reference to a committee, unless for good cause shown, and by unanimous consent of all the members present.

To deliver Lectures appertaining to the Degrees.

SEC. 16. The several Lodges under this jurisdiction shall in all cases of conferring degrees, deliver at the time, the lecture appertaining to the degree conferred.

Rights of Delegates of Lodges under Dispensation.

SEC. 17. Delegates of Lodges under Dispensation shall be allowed to take seats in the Grand Lodge and participate in the discussions, but not to vote, or serve on committees, or hold office therein.

Lodges cannot appear in Public Procession.

SEC. 18. No Lodge under this jurisdiction shall appear in public procession as Masons on any other than purely Masonic occasions.

Avouchment for Visitors.

SEC. 19. To prevent evil consequences, the Masters of constituent Lodges will permit no Mason to vouch for a Brother when visiting a Lodge, without having sat in open Lodge with him or examined him under the sanction or authority of the Master.

---

*Resolved, That in the Annual Lodge Returns, Secretaries must invariably report the *full given name* of each member. (Adopted 1874).

Diplomas.

SEC. 20. Any Master Mason under this jurisdiction, in good and regular standing, upon the presentation of a certificate to that effect to the Grand Secretary, shall (upon the payment of three dollars), be entitled to have his Diploma authenticated in due form.

Members of Constituent Lodges in arrears for dues—When to Suspend.

SEC. 21. Any member of a Lodge being twelve months in arrears for dues, and residing within the jurisdiction of this Grand Lodge, shall be notified by the Secretary that unless within thirty days, or if residing without the jurisdiction of this Grand Lodge, within sixty days from the date of the regular meeting at which such delinquency shall be made known to the Lodge, either his dues be paid, or sickness or inability to pay be shown as the cause of such refusal or neglect, he will be liable to suspension from all the rights and privileges of Masonry. If neither of the foregoing excuses be made, he may at the first regular meeting after the expiration of the specified time, be declared by the Master to be suspended, unless for special reasons shown, the Lodge shall remit his dues or grant him further time for payment. But any Mason thus suspended, who shall at any time pay the arrearages due at the time of his suspension, or who shall have such arrearages remitted by his Lodge, shall be declared by the Master thereof restored.

Dues cannot be charged during Suspension.

SEC. 22. When a Mason is suspended for any cause whatever, he is, for the time of such suspension, debarred from all the rights and privileges of Masonry, and no dues shall be collected of him during the time of such suspension.

UNIFORMITY OF WORK.

Board of Custodians.

SEC. 23. There shall be a Committee on Work, composed of the Grand Lecturer, who shall be, *ex officio*, Chairman, and three members of the Grand Lodge, to be appointed by the Grand Master, as provided for in Section 6 of these By-Laws, to serve as a Board of Custodians during the year, whose duty it shall be to preserve the Standard Work of this Grand Lodge and see that the same is faithfully practiced in all the constituent Lodges in this jurisdiction.*

Masters must have the Work exemplified—Employment of Grand Lecturer.

SEC. 24. It shall be the duty of the Master of each Lodge in this jurisdiction, to cause the work, as adopted by this Grand Lodge, to be exemplified by the Grand Lecturer at least once a year, and for that purpose he shall cause to be convened a Lodge of Instruction, and invite the Grand Lecturer to be present thereat and teach the work; and the Lodge, he is so instructing, shall pay him a reasonable amount for his time and expenses.

*Standing Resolution: *Resolved,* "That any member of the Board of Custodians shall, after the adoption of the work by them, have authority to enforce said work in all Lodges in this jurisdiction." (Adopted Nov 15th, 1877.)

5

COMMITTEES.

Their Duties.

SEC. 25. The duties of the several Committees are as follows :

First, On Credentials: This Committee shall receive and examine the credentials of the Representatives to the Grand Lodge and report thereon as soon as practicable after its opening.

Second, On Grand Master's Address: To this Committee shall be referred the Annual Address of the Grand Master for comment and distribution.

Third, On Grievance and Appeals: To this Committee shall be referred all grievances between members of the Grand Lodge while in session, and they shall examine all trial records sent from Lodges to the Grand Lodge as provided for in Section 4 of the Trial Code and report thereon.

Fourth, On Finance: This Committee shall examine into and report upon the financial reports of the Grand Officers, and all matters touching the finances of the Grand Lodge, and to whom shall be referred all subjects involving an appropriation of the Grand Lodge funds; and without such reference and report no appropriation of money shall be made.

Fifth, On Grand Lodge Library: This Committee shall examine the annual report of the Grand Librarian and the condition of the Library. It is expected that the Committee will make and advance all necessary suggestions for the best interest and furtherance of the Library.

Sixth, On Lodges under Dispensation: To this Committee shall be referred the record and other books of Lodges U. D., and all cases of forfeited charters. They shall not act upon any application for a charter, unless they shall have found the work in accordance with the Laws of this Grand Lodge.

Seventh, On Returns of Chartered Lodges: To this Committee shall be referred the returns of members, etc., and dues of chartered Lodges; it shall carefully examine into their correctness and adjust the same. The Committee shall also report upon the By-Laws of chartered Lodges, and point out any want of conformity to the Laws of this Grand Lodge

Eighth, On Unfinished Business: This Committee shall carefully examine the printed transactions of the previous Communcation and report all unfinished business.

Ninth, On Jurisprudence: To this Committee shall be referred all domestic correspondence requiring action, and questions relative to the usages, privileges, customs and work of the Fraternity. To this Committee shall also be referred all propositions to amend the Constitution and Laws of the Grand Lodge.

Tenth, On Correspondence: To this Committee shall be referred immediately after their receipt by the Grand Secretary, all printed Proceedings of sister Grand Lodges, and all foreign Communications, and such miscellaneous matter, as may not otherwise be specially disposed of. The Committee is required to submit its report at the next succeeding annual Communication.

No Action without Report from Proper Committee.

SEC. 26. No business of any kind shall be finally acted upon until after

SECTION 25. Subdivision *Fifth*, On Grand Lodge Library:

To this Committee shall be referred the annual report of the Grand Librarian. It shall carefully examine the same and make all necessary suggestions for the best interests of the Library. The Committee shall, in connection with the Grand Librarian, have charge of the Library, make such purchases of books, as in their judgment may seem advisable, and generally do all things which may promote the best interests of the Library, provided no debt shall be incurred thereby. (Masonic Code, page 18.)

reference to and report upon by the proper Committee, unless by unanimous consent of the Grand Lodge.

MISCELLANEOUS.

Representatives of Lodges shall wear their Jewels in Grand Lodge.

SEC. 27. Members of the Grand Lodge, not Officers therein, Representatives of constituent Lodges, shall appear at its Annual Communications, clothed with the Jewels which they are entitled to wear in their respective Lodges.

Trial Code to Govern.

SEC. 28. Masonic Crimes, Trials and Punishments for the same, Restorations and Appeals shall be governed by the Trial Code, adopted by this Grand Lodge and published herewith.

AMENDMENTS.

How made—Two-Thirds Vote necessary.

SEC. 29. No amendment to these By-Laws shall be adopted, unless it has been referred to the Committee on Jurisprudence; and by a two-thirds vote of all the members present in Annual Communication.

RULES REGULATING BUSINESS

OF THE

Most Worshipful Grand Lodge

OF

Ancient, Free and Accepted Masons of Utah.

Grand Master governs—Penalty.

RULE 1. At the first stroke of the Grand Master's gavel, there shall be a general silence, and he who breaks silence, without leave from the Chair, shall be subject to a general reprimand. Under the same penalty, every Brother shall keep his seat and observe strict silence whenever the Grand Master or presiding officer shall call to order.

Restriction in Debate.

RULE 2. No Brother is to speak more than once on the same question, unless by permission.

To obey Rules—Penalty.

RULE 3. If, in the Grand Lodge, any member is twice called to order, at one Communication, for transgressing these rules, and is guilty of the third offense of the same nature, the Chair may peremptorily order him to leave the Lodge room for that day.

Ridicule not permissible—Penalty.

RULE 4. Whoever shall be so rude as to ridicule a Brother, or what another says, or has said, may be forthwith solemnly excluded from the Communication and declared incapable of ever being a member of the Grand Lodge for the future, unless he publicly own his fault and be excused.

Motions to be decided by Majority.

RULE 5. All motions are to be decided by a majority of votes, each member having one vote, each Lodge having three votes and the Grand Master having the casting vote in case of a tie.

Grand Marshal and Deacons permitted to walk around.

RULE 6. All members shall keep their seats except the Grand Marshal and Grand Deacons, who are allowed to move from place to place in the discharge of their duties.

To adaress Grand Master and keep Decorum.

RULE 7. Everyone who speaks shall arise and remain standing, addressing himself to the Most Worshipful Grand Master, and no member shall interrupt him, unless to call him to order; but after he has been set right he may proceed, if he observe due order and decorum.

Committees not to sit during Sessions.

RULE 8. The Standing Committees shall not sit while the Grand Lodge is actually in session, unless on leave obtained.

Order of Business First Session.

RULE 9. After the Grand Master has called the Grand Lodge to order on the first day of the Annual Communication, the following order of business and proceedings shall be observed:

1. Calling the roll of the Grand Officers and Lodges by the Grand Secretary.
2. The usual solemn ceremonies of opening the Grand Lodge in *ample form.*
3. Prayer by the Grand Chaplain.
4. Reading and approving the Minutes of any previous Communication not before read and approved.
5. Report of Committee on Credentials.
6. Appointment by the Grand Master of the Regular Committees.
7. Address by the Grand Master and action thereon.
8. Report of the Deputy Grand Master and action thereon.
9. Reports of the Grand Treasurer and Grand Secretary and action thereon.
10. Reports of Committees appointed at the previous Annual Communication with instructions to report at the present Communication.
11. Miscellaneous business.

Order of Business at Second and Succeeding Sessions.

RULE 10. After the order of business provided in Rule 9, shall have been finished, the daily order of business during the Annual Communication, shall be as follows:

1. Reading and approving Minutes of the preceding session.
2. Reports of unfinished business of previous Communications and sessions
3. Presentation and reference or other disposition of Memorials, Petitions and Communications.
4. Motions and Resolutions, and reference or other disposition of the same.
5. Reports of Regular and Standing Committees, and action thereon; the Committee on Correspondence and Masonic Jurisprudence having the preference.
6. Reports of Special Committees, and action thereon.
7. Special Orders.

6

8. Unfinished Business of the previous session.

9, Miscellaneous Business not included in the above.

Further Order of Business.

RULE 11. Should the order of business not be concluded at the session at which it is first called, it shall be commenced at the succeeding session, where it was left off, and so on throughout the Communication, taking up the order of business as in Rule 10.

Reports of Committees—How to be made—Chairman.

RULE 12. All reports of Committees of the Grand Lodge shall be reduced to writing in a legible hand, on one side only of legal cap and signed at least by a majority of the Committee. The first named Brother on each Committee is Chairman.

To be reduced to Writing.

RULE 13. Every resolution or motion submitted to the Grand Lodge shall, if required, be reduced to writing and referred to an appropriate Committee.

Motion, when debatable.

RULE 14. No motion shall be debatable until seconded, and stated from the chair, when it shall be in possession of the Grand Lodge and cannot be withdrawn, except by the mover, previous to decision or amendment. A question, after being put by the Grand Master, cannot be debated.

Motion to close &c. inadmissible.

RULE 15. No motion to close or call off is admissible, that responsibility resting alone with the Grand Master, who is obligated to allow the occurrence of nothing tending to interrupt or defeat the regular course of any business legitimately coming before the Grand Lodge.

Parliamentary Rules—Previous Question.

RULE 16. On all other matters, the rules which govern deliberative assemblies shall be observed, except as to the previous question.

Reconsideration of Votes.

RULE 17. No vote of the Grand Lodge shall be reconsidered by a less number of members than were present at the passing of the same.

Two-Thirds Vote required to suspend.

RULE 18. These Rules of Order shall not be suspended at any time, unless by a vote of two-thirds of the members present.

Two-Thirds Vote required to amend.

RULE 19. These Rules may be amended at any time by a vote of two-thirds of the members of the Grand Lodge present.

STANDING ORDERS AND RESOLUTIONS

OF THE

MOST WORSHIPFUL GRAND LODGE

OF

ANCIENT, FREE AND ACCEPTED MASONS OF UTAH.

---

1. *Resolved*, That all Masons belonging to Lodges in this jurisdiction are forbidden to hold any Masonic intercourse with any Mason belonging to a Lodge under the jurisdiction of the Grand Lodge of Hamburg, or to any Lodge holding a charter from said Grand Lodge, and any Brother doing so shall be subject to the highest Masonic penalties. January, 1872, p. 14.

2. *Resolved*, That all Masons belonging to Lodges in this jurisdiction are forbidden to hold any Masonic intercourse with any Mason belonging to any Lodge under the jurisdiction of the Grand Orient of France, or to any Lodge holding a charter from the said Grand Orient of France, and any Brother doing so shall be subject to the highest Masonic penalties. January, 1872, p. 14.

3. *Resolved*, That it shall be the duty of each Master to have the printed Proceedings of the Grand Lodge read in open Lodge, that no Brother can plead ignorance of the Proceedings of the Grand Lodge. October, 1872, p. 27.

4. *Resolved*, That when there are two or more Lodges holding concurrent jurisdiction, the jurisdiction over non affiliated and non-resident Masons shall be exercised by individual Lodges, turn about. *Provided*, That when a particular Lodge may desire to exercise jurisdiction out of turn, it may do so with the consent of two-thirds of the Lodges interested. October, 1872, p. 27.

5. *Resolved*, That a candidate who has once been rejected by a Lodge within this jurisdiction shall not apply for the degrees to any other Lodge, without the consent of a majority of the members present at a regular meeting of the Lodge which rejected him. 1873, p. 32

6. *Resolved*, That each constituent Lodge in this jurisdiction is required to procure and keep a Lodge Register, the blank spaces of which shall correspond with the Grand Lodge Register, and that the Grand Secretary is requested to forward to each Lodge a blank form to be used as a pattern for their Register. 1873, p. 33.

7. *Resolved*, That the Grand Secretary be, and he is hereby required to procure for the use, and at the expense of the constituent Lodges, two bound volumes of the Proceedings of each Annual Communication of this Grand Lodge, which shall be for the use of the Officers and members, and shall be retained at all times within the Lodge. 1873, p. 36.

8. *Resolved*, That each Lodge within this jurisdiction shall enter the Quarterly Notice of the Grand Secretary in a book to be known as the "Black Book." Said book shall be so arranged as to show, in alphabetical order and by appropriate columns, the names of the persons, name and number of Lodge, date of rejection, suspension or expulsion, as the case may be, the cause therefor, and the date of re instatement when notified thereof. 1873, p. 36.

9. *Resolved*, That the Grand Secretary be empowered to sell copies of the Proceedings of this Grand Lodge to members of this jurisdiction at one dollar each, the proceeds of which shall be appropriated to the benefit of the Library, and that the Grand Secretary shall keep a separate account of all funds pertaining to the Library. 1873, p. 37.

10. *Resolved*, That in the Annual Lodge Returns, Secretaries must invariably report the *full given name* of each member. 1874, p. 47.

11. *Resolved*, That all non-affiliated Masons in this jurisdiction shall have the privilege of visiting Lodges for the period of six months, but such Non-affiliates shall petition some Lodge within thirty days thereafter for membership, or contribute to some chartered Lodge in this Jurisdiction its regular dues, and in case of non-compliance, shall be debarred from all Masonic rights and privileges, as follows:

1st.   They shall not be allowed to visit any Lodge.

2d.   They shall not be allowed to appear in any Masonic procession.

3d.   They shall not be entitled to Masonic charity.

4th.   They shall not be entitled to Masonic burial.

They shall be deemed drones in the hive of Masonry, and unworthy our protection as Masons.

And be it further *resolved*, that this resolution shall be printed on the back of each dimit granted in this jurisdiction. 1874, p. 48.

12. *Resolved*, That it shall be the duty of all Lodges within this jurisdiction to punish, by reprimand, suspension or expulsion, all members who may be found guilty of drunkenness or gambling. 1874, p. 50.

13. *Resolved*, That hereafter no Brother shall be appointed or installed to any office in this Grand Lodge, unless he is entitled to a seat therein, as per Report of the Committee on Credentials, except the Grand Tyler. 1874, p. 56.

14. *Resolved*, That hereafter Elective Officers shall not be installed by proxy. 1875, p. 33.

15. *Resolved*, That this Grand Lodge recommends to constituent Lodges in this jurisdiction, the establishment of Life Membership, at the uniform fee of one hundred dollars, which shall thereafter exempt the Brother, taking such Life Membership, from all Lodge dues. 1876, p. 37.

STANDING RESOLUTION, NO. 20.

Resolved, That it shall be the duty of the Secretary of each Lodge in this Jurisdiction to include in his annual return to the Grand Secretary, the name of every member who has died during the year, together with such particulars of his life and traits of character as are worthy of commemoration, which facts shall be communicated to the Grand Lodge by the Grand Secretary in his annual report.

(Masonic Code, page 25.)

16. *Resolved*, That any member of the Board of Custodians shall, after the adoption of the work by them, have authority to enforce said work in all Lodges in this Grand jurisdiction. 1877, p. 34.

17. *Resolved*, That it is the duty of a member of any Lodge in this Grand Jurisdiction, objecting to the advancement of an Entered Apprentice or Fellow Craft, to prefer charges against the Brother at the next regular meeting of the Lodge; and if he fails to do so, the degree may be conferred. 1878, p. 43.

18. *Resolved*, That any Master Mason, residing in Utah, and hailing from a Grand Jurisdiction where no dimits are issued to members, may petition any Lodge in this Grand Jurisdiction for affiliation without an accompanying dimit, *providing* he produces other satisfactory evidence that he is a Master Mason in good standing. 1878, p. 43.

19. *Resolved*, That the testimony of the wife of either the complainant or accused shall not be competent in Masonic Trials in this Grand Jurisdiction. 1878, p. 43.

APPROVED DECISIONS OF GRAND MASTERS

OF THE

MOST WORSHIPFUL GRAND LODGE

OF

ANCIENT, FREE AND ACCEPTED MASONS OF UTAH.

AFFILIATION.

Applicants for affiliation have the right to apply to any Lodge they may choose, at any time after their rejection.—*Robertson*, 1873, p. 8—Jur. Com., p. 52.

BY-LAWS.

A Brother raised in a Lodge, or elected to become a member thereof by affiliation, must sign its By-Laws, and a contumacious refusal to sign, after having made himself thoroughly conversant with their provisions, should be made the subject of Masonic discipline.—*Robertson*, 1873, p. 8—Jur. Com., p. 41.

CHARTER.

The officers in authority at the time of the issuance of a Charter must sign it.—*Robertson*, 1873, p. 8.

DIMITS.

Dimits accompanying a petition for a charter are the property of the Grand Lodge, and must be retained by the Grand Secretary.—*Robertson*, 1873, p. 8.

DISPLAYS.

Masonic displays, on any other than purely Masonic occasions, are not permissible.—*Johnson*, 1876, p. 11.

FEES.

The fees accompanying a petition for initiation become the property of the Lodge the moment they are paid into the hands of the Secretary. It is his duty to receive all moneys due the Lodge, and pay them over to the Treasurer immediately. The fee for initiation is money due the Lodge, for without it the petition

A Junior Warden has the right to preside over the Lodge in the absence of the Master and Senior Warden, but is not entitled to fill the position in his absence, he may be assigned to it by courtesy of the Master. (Masonic Code, page 27, Subhead "Officers.")

The application of an Entered Apprentice or Fellow Craft, who has received one or both of the degrees in a Lodge of a Sister Grand Jurisdiction must be accompanied by a certificate, under the seal of the original Lodge, waiving jurisdiction; the application must then be referred to a Committee of Investigation and proceeded with, as in all other cases of petition for the three degrees. On signing the By-Laws, the Brother becomes a member of the Lodge conferring the M∴ M∴ degree upon him. (Masonic Code, page 27, subhead, "Petitions.")

should not be received. In case of rejection of the petition, the order drawn upon the Treasurer is lasting evidence that the money has been returned.—*Scott*, 1878, p. 11.

JURISDICTION.

The jurisdiction of a Lodge over a rejected candidate is perpetual. The petition of a person for the degrees in Masonry, who has previously been rejected, should not be received without the consent of the Lodge rejecting him, and the applicant having moved into a foreign jurisdiction strengthens rather than weakens this rule.—*Orr*, 1877, p 7.

MINUTES.

The names of Investigating Committees on petitions must be recorded in the minutes of the evening.—*Bennett*, 1875, p. 8.

MOTIONS.

The Master rules and governs the Lodge, and may refuse any motion deemed by him frivolous or impolitic.—*Scott*, 1878, p. 11.

NOTICE OF SUSPENSION

A Secretary of a Lodge need not inform a Chapter or Commandery of the suspension or expulsion of a member who is supposed to be a member of these Bodies. But the Secretary would be careless of his duty, if he knew of a particular Lodge the suspended or expelled Mason was in the habit of visiting, and did not inform it.—*Orr*, 1877, p. 8.

OBJECTION.

Objection to the advancement of an Entered Apprentice or Fellow Craft is not valid when made by a Mason not a member of the Lodge, unless the objecting Brother prefers charges.—*Scott*, 1878, p. 12.

OFFICERS.

Elective Officers of a Lodge can neither resign nor dimit until the end of the Masonic year for which they were elected.—*Orr*, 1877, p. 9.

PAST MASTER'S DEGREE.

A Master elect must receive the Past Master's Degree from three actual Masters, or Past Masters, before he can be installed.—*Cohn*, 1877, p. 11.

PETITION.

Brothers recommending a petition for the Degrees, or for Affiliation, must be members of the Lodge to which the application is made.—*Orr*, 1877, p. 9.

PHYSICAL QUALIFICATIONS.

A Lodge can receive the petition of a person who has lost one eye—the other being sound and healthy. The old regulation relating to the deformity of applicants is greatly relaxed, and justly so.—*Orr*, 1877, p. 7.

RESTORATION.

A suspended Mason may petition the Lodge, that suspended him, for restoration without withdrawing his appeal to the Grand Lodge, the fact of restoration would not necessarily invalidate his appeal, as the Grand Lodge might conclude that the sentence was unjust or the punishment unwarranted, while restoration may have been granted from merciful motives. Should it be refused after the appeal has been withdrawn, the Brother would have no redress.—*Scott*, 1878, p. 12.

The *status* of a Brother holding membership in a sister jurisdiction, who has been suspended and subsequently restored in this jurisdiction is that of a non-affiliate, with the right to apply to be re-instated in his mother Lodge or any other he may choose. A certificate of restoration should be granted by the Lodge which restores him.—*Scott*, 1878, p. 12.

RIGHTS TO SIT IN LODGE PENDING CHARGES.

A Brother has the right to sit in a Lodge while charges are pending against him. It is simply a matter of his own taste and discretion.—*Bennett*, 1876, p. 8.

SUMMONS.

Summonses should be issued *sparingly*. A willful disregard of a Lodge summons is a Masonic offense, and a Brother guilty of it should be disciplined.—*Cohn*, 1874, p. 8.

VISITORS.

The Worshipful Master has the right to request visiting Brethren to retire, if he has private business before his Lodge.—*Bennett*, 1875, p. 8.

VOTE.

~~All members of a Lodge present must vote when a ballot is spread, whether in arrears for dues or not, and it is the duty of the Worshipful Master to see that they do vote.—*Orr*, 1877, p. 9.~~

WORK.

The Master, nor even the Master and Wardens, have no right to request the Master of a sister Lodge to confer the E. A., or any other degree in Masonry upon the material of their Lodge, without the consent of the Lodge. It is the duty of every Lodge in the jurisdiction to do its own work.—*Orr*, 1877, p. 8.

Lodges cannot assemble for work on the Sabbath. The only meetings of the Lodge appropriate to that day are such as are held for the purpose of attending the funeral of a deceased Brother.—*Scott*, 1878, p. 11.

TRIAL CODE

OF THE

MOST WORSHIPFUL GRAND LODGE

OF

ANCIENT, FREE AND ACCEPTED MASONS OF UTAH.

Resolved, That the following "Trial Code" be adopted and promulgated for the government of this Grand Lodge and the constituent Lodges in this Grand Jurisdiction.*

Offenses punishable.

SECTION 1. Masonic crimes are defined to be:

First—A violation of any of the duties enjoined by the Ancient Charges.

Second—The doing of any act contrary to, or subversive of, the three great duties which the Mason owes to God, his neighbor and himself.

Third—Conduct which tends to impair the unsullied purity of the Fraternity, or which is, in any wise, contrary to the obligations and the written teachings of the Institution.

Fourth—Members in arrears for dues may be dealt with agreeable to Section 21 of the By-Laws of this Grand Lodge.

Rules to Govern Trial.

SEC. 2. Whenever a member of a Lodge, or a Brother, residing or sojourning in this jurisdiction, shall be accused of any offense, which, if proved, would subject him to reprimand, suspension or expulsion, the proceedings in the premises shall be conducted substantially agreeably to the following Rules:

Charges—How Made and Disposed of—Election of Commissioners.

Rule 1. All charges for un-Masonic conduct shall be made in writing, signed by the accuser, specifying, with reasonable certainty, the character of the offense alleged, and delivered to the Secretary at a regular meeting of the Lodge, who

*Adopted in Grand Lodge Nov. 12th, 1874.

8

shall then read it and enter it in full on the minutes. At the next regular meeting it shall be the duty of the Worshipful Master to cause to be elected by ballot, and by a majority of those present, six of its members, who shall assemble as Commissioners to hear and determine thereupon, at such time and place, convenient to the parties, as he shall indicate.

How to Serve Notice—*Ex parte Trial—To Appoint Attorney.*

Rule 2.—If the residence of the accused is known, and within thirty miles of the place where the Lodge having the matter in charge is located, the accused shall be entitled to a personal service ten days before trial. If the residence of the accused be a greater distance than thirty miles, but within the jurisdiction, then and in that case, a summons to appear and answer, forwarded to him by mail or other conveyance, twenty days before the trial, shall be considered sufficient. If his residence be out of the jurisdiction and known, and more than thirty miles distant, then the summons shall be issued thirty days before the trial. If his residence be unknown, or he neglect or refuse to obey the summons, when service has been had, the Lodge shall proceed *ex parte*, the Worshipful Master having first appointed some Brother to act as the attorney of the accused, and conduct the proceedings to a final determination.

Who may Prefer Charges.

Rule 3.—When any member of a Lodge (except its Master or the Grand Master), or any Mason residing within the jurisdiction, shall be accused of un-Masonic conduct, charges to that effect may be preferred by any Master Mason in good standing. But to further the administration of justice, it is made the especial duty of the Junior Warden, in the absence of other accusers, to prefer all charges for offenses committed when the Lodge is not at labor; but the neglect or refusal of the Junior Warden to perform such duty shall not prevent any other Brother from preferring and prosecuting any charge of un-Masonic conduct which may come to his knowledge.

Offenses in Open Lodge—How to Deal with.

Rule 4.—In all instances where offenses are committed while the Lodge is at labor, the foregoing rules, requiring notice and delay, may be dispensed with, and the Worshipful Master is authorized to order the offending Brother to show cause *instanter*, why he shall not be promptly dealt with.

Jurisdiction of Lodge—To Notify Lodge of Accused.

Rule 5.—Every Lodge has jurisdiction over its own members, and all Non-Affiliated Masons residing or sojourning in its jurisdiction. If the offender hold membership in another Lodge, the charge shall be sent to that Lodge for trial, but if such Lodge refuse or waive the right to entertain the charge, then, and in that case, the Lodge under whose jurisdiction the offense was committed shall proceed to the trial of the accused as provided in Section II, Rule 1.

How to Conduct Trial—Testimony—Counsel—Ten Days to Conclude.

Rule 6.—The Commissioners shall assemble at the time and place appointed, and shall be presided over by the Worshipful Master, who shall decide all questions of Masonic Law which may arise during the trial. These meetings of the Commissioners shall also be attended by the Junior Warden, who shall act as Prosecuting Attorney for the Lodge, and by the Secretary, or some other member of the Lodge appointed for that purpose by the Worshipful Master, who shall keep a correct and full record of the proceedings of the trial. The Worshipful Master shall, at the request of either party, summon such witnesses as are Masons, residing within the jurisdiction of his Lodge, to appear and testify before the Commissioners. Whenever the attendance of a witness, who is a Mason, and who resides without the jurisdiction of the Lodge in which the trial is had, cannot be procured, his testimony may be taken before the Worshipful Master of the Lodge within whose jurisdiction he resides, upon such notice to the adverse party as the Worshipful Master of the Lodge in which the trial is to be had shall fix, and the attendance of such witness may be compelled by summons. His testimony shall be reduced to writing, signed by him, and authenticated by the certificate of the Worshipful Master before whom it is taken, under the seal of his Lodge. The testimony of witnesses who are not Masons shall be taken by deposition before some officer authorized by the laws of the State wherein he resides to administer oaths, and at such time and place, and upon such notice to the adverse party as shall be designated by the Worshipful Master, upon the application of the party desiring the testimony. Whenever the testimony of a witness residing out of this Territory is desired, it shall be taken upon interrogatories, direct and cross, agreed upon by the parties or settled by the Worshipful Master. Witnesses who are Masons in good standing shall testify upon their honor as such; and all others shall testify under oath or affirmation.* Any Master Mason in good standing may, at the request of the accuser or the accused, appear as his counsel and assist in the prosecution or defense. The Commissioners may adjourn from time to time, at their own convenience or for sufficient cause shown by either party; provided, that the period within which their duties shall be concluded shall not exceed ten days, unless, for good reasons shown, the Worshipful Master shall grant them further time.

Commissioners to Pronounce Verdict and Sentence—Two-Thirds Vote Required.

Rule 7. After all the testimony shall have been received the Commissioners shall proceed to deliberate upon their verdict and sentence, with none present save themselves. The judgment of two-thirds of the Commissioners shall be taken as the decision of the whole. Their decision and finding shall be final and shall, signed by them all, be presented to the Worshipful Master, who at the next regular meeting of the Lodge, shall pronounce the result, and direct the Secretary to record the same as the judgment of the Lodge and file the record for safe keeping among its archives.

*Standing Resolution, adopted Nov. 13th, 1878: Resolved, That the testimony of the wife of either the complainant or accused shall not be competent in Masonic Trials in this Jurisdiction.

Penalty—When Sentence takes Effect—Notice to Person and Grand Secretary.

SEC. 3.   The penalties which may be inflicted, are reprimand in open Lodge, suspension or expulsion. If the sentence be reprimand, the Worshipful Master shall summon the adjudged to appear at the next regular meeting, when it shall be carried into effect. If it be suspension or expulsion, it shall at once go into effect, and the Secretary shall immediately notify the person suspended or expelled and the Grand Secretary thereof.

Appeal—How Made—To Transmit Trial Record to Grand Secretary.

SEC. 4.   An appeal may be taken to the Grand Lodge by either party at its next succeeding Annual Communication, but not unless a notice of such intended appeal shall have been given to the Worshipful Master in writing, within thirty days after his announcement of the result of the trial. In all appealed cases and in all cases of expulsion or suspension, whether appealed or not, the Worshipful Master shall cause the Secretary to prepare a transcipt of the record of trial, and immediately transmit it to the Grand Secretary, together with information of the appeal intended, if any there be.

To Transmit Trial Record to Grand Secretary to be Examined by Grand Lodge— Its Decision is Final.

SEC. 5   All judgments from which an appeal shall be taken, and all transcripts of trial-records where the punishment is expulsion or suspension, shall be sent to the Grand Secretary at least thirty days prior to the Annual Communication, and shall be reviewed in the Grand Lodge, or before a Committee thereof, during its session, upon the record sent up and upon such other proper documents as may be submitted, and the Grand Lodge may affirm, modify or reverse the judgment of the Lodge, or may make such other order relative thereto as shall be deemed proper and its decision shall be final and conclusive.

Time of Suspension—How Restoration may take Place in Lodge—Two-Thirds Vote—Notice to Grand Secretary and Restored Party.

SEC. 6.   All sentences of suspension shall be for a definite or an indefinite period, at the option of the Commission. If definite, the Commission shall fix the duration of the same; and after the sentence has been announced the Secretary shall inform the Grand Secretary thereof, together with the period of suspension. If indefinite the Lodge may at any regular meeting, by the votes of two-thirds of the members present, annul any such sentence of suspension pronounced by itself, and restore the Mason thus suspended to all his Masonic rights and privileges; *provided* that notice of a resolution for such restoration shall have been given at the regular meeting next preceding. In all cases of restoration the Secretary shall notify the restored party and the Grand Secretary thereof.

Grand Lodge may Restore to Rights of Masonry but not Membership—Entitled to Certificate.

SEC. 7.   The Grand Lodge may, at any Annual Communication, if good cause therefor be shown and proof be given of the notice hereinafter prescribed,

restore to the rights and privileges of Masonry a Mason who has been suspended or expelled within its jurisdiction; but such restoration shall not restore him to membership in the Lodge by which he was suspended or expelled; but he shall receive from the Grand Secretary a certificate under the seal of the Grand Lodge, showing his good standing.

Suspended Mason—How to Apply to Grand Lodge for Restoration—Forty Days Notice.

SEC. 8.   Whenever any Mason, suspended for un-Masonic conduct desires to petition the Grand Lodge for restoration to the rights and privileges of Masonry, he shall first make application for such restoration to the Lodge by which he was suspended, if it still be in existence.   If his application be there refused, it may then be made to the Grand Lodge, provided that notice in writing, be given to the Lodge of such intended application, not less than forty days preceding the Annual Communication.

Expelled Mason—How to Apply to Grand Lodge for Restoration—Sixty Days Notice.

SEC. 9.   Whenever any expelled Mason desires to petition the Grand Lodge for restoration to the rights and privileges of Masonry, he shall, in writing, notify the Lodge which expelled him, if it still be in existence, of his intention so to do, at least sixty days before the Annual Communication at which his petition is to be presented, accompanying said notice with a copy of intended petition; and before said petition shall be considered by the Grand Lodge, proof of the giving of said notice to the Lodge shall be furnished.

ARRAIGNMENT OF MASTER.

Cause for and how to Prefer Charges.

SECTION 1.   Charges may be preferred against the Master of a Lodge for abuse of his power, violation of the Constitution or Regulations, or for un-Masonic conduct of any kind, by any three Master Masons in good standing; which charges shall be in writing over their signatures, and shall be presented to the Grand Lodge, if in session, or to the Grand Master during vacation.

Grand Master to Appoint Commissioners—Summons—Time to Answer.

SEC. 2.   Upon the presentation of such charges, the Grand Lodge, or the Grand Master, as the case may be, may at once appoint and summon not less than three nor more than seven disinterested Masters to assemble as Commissioners to hear and determine thereupon, and shall then summon the accused to appear and answer thereunto, at such time and place most convenient for the parties, as shall

9

be indicated in said summons, giving him, if within the jurisdiction at least ten days—if without the jurisdiction at least sixty days—to answer thereunto; and transmitting him also a copy of the charges.

Witnesses—How to Take Evidence.

Sec. 3.   The Commissioners thus assembled shall choose one of their number to preside, and one to act as Secretary, and the member presiding shall have the authority to summon witnesses at the request of either party; the witnesses, if Masons, shall testify upon their honor as such; if not, their depositions shall be taken in writing before an officer legally authorized to administer oaths, and in such case the party requiring such depositions shall notify the other of the time and place they will be taken, that he may, if he choose, be present thereat.

Time of Trial Limited.

Sec. 4.   The Commissioners may adjourn, from time to time, at their own convenience, or for good cause shown by either party: *provided,* That the period within which their duties shall be concluded shall not exceed ten days, unless for sufficient reasons the Grand Master shall grant them further time.

Judgment—How Determined.

Sec. 5.   The opinion of a majority of the Commissioners shall be deemed the judgment of the whole and shall be conclusive, unless an appeal be taken at the next Annual Communication of the Grand Lodge.

Commissioners to Inflict Penalty.

Sec. 6.   The penalties which may be inflicted by such Commissioners may be either deprivation of office, suspension or expulsion, as in their judgment shall be deemed proper.

To Keep Record and Transmit to Grand Secretary.

Sec. 7.   The Commissioners shall keep a complete record of their proceedings and of their judgment, and shall transmit the same to the Grand Secretary at the conclusion of the trial, and the judgment shall be at once carried into effect by order of the Grand Master.

Appeal—When Taken.

Sec. 8.   An appeal to the Grand Lodge may be taken at its next Annual Communication, by either party, if notice thereof be given to the Grand Secretary, within thirty days after the conclusion of the trial.

Uniform Code of By-Laws

For the Government of Constituent Lodges under the Jurisdiction

of the

Most Worshipful Grand Lodge

of

Ancient, Free and Accepted Masons of Utah.

Resolved, That the following "Uniform Code of By-Laws" is recommended for adoption to the constituent Lodges in this Grand Jurisdiction, but such Lodges may adopt additions, which shall not be inconsistent with the Constitution, By-Laws, and Rules and Regulations of this Grand Lodge, to meet local circumstances.*:

By-Laws

—of—

.............Lodge, No..........., Ancient Free and Accepted Masons.

ARTICLE I.

The Lodge—Its Title and Warrant.

SECTION 1.   The title of this Lodge shall be——, No.——.

SEC. 2.   The warrant of this Lodge is a Charter, granted on the——day of——, A. D. 18— by the Most Worshipful Grand Lodge of Ancient, Free and Accepted Masons of Utah, to whose Constitutional Rules and Edicts the most explicit respect and obedience shall ever be paid by its members.

*Adopted in Grand Lodge, November 12th, A. D. 1872.

ARTICLE II.

Meetings.

SECTION 1. The regular meetings of this Lodge shall be holden on the——in each month.

SEC. 2. Special meetings may be called from time to time, as the Lodge, or the Worshipful Master thereof, may direct.

SEC. 3. The hour of meeting from———shall be————,and from————to————shall be————.

SEC. 4. This Lodge shall be represented at each Annual Communication of the Grand Lodge of Utah, as far as possible.

ARTICLE III.

Petitions and Membership.

SECTION 1. All petitions for initiation or affiliation must be signed by the petitioner and be recommended by two members of the Lodge. Every such petition shall be referred to a committee of three, whose duty it shall be to report thereon at the regular meeting one lunar month thereafter (unless further time be granted), when the applicant may be balloted for and received or rejected, or the ballot may be postponed until the ensuing regular meeting, as the Lodge may determine.

SEC. 2. If an applicant elected to receive the Degrees in this Lodge does not come forward to be initiated within three months thereafter, the fee shall be forfeited, unless the Lodge shall otherwise direct.

SEC. 3. After a petition for the Degrees or affiliation has been referred to a Committee it cannot be withdrawn, unless for good cause shown.

SEC. 4. Every person raised to the degree of Master Mason in, or elected a member of this Lodge, shall sign the By-Laws thereof.

SEC. 5. The members of this Lodge are all who have been or may be raised or elected therein, and who have subscribed their names to its By-Laws.

ARTICLE IV.

The Officers, their Election and Installation.

SECTION 1. The Officers of this Lodge shall consist of a Worshipful Master, a Senior Warden, a Junior Warden, a Treasurer, a Secretary, a Senior Deacon, a Junior Deacon, two Stewards, a Tyler and three Trustees.

SEC. 2. The Worshipful Master, Senior Warden, Junior Warden, Treasurer, Secretary and Trustees, shall be elected by ballot, all other officers shall be appointed by the Worshipful Master immediately after his installation, except the Junior Deacon who may be appointed by the Senior Warden.

SEC. 3. At the regular meeting preceding St. John's Day, in December of each year the election of Officers shall be held in the following manner: The

Secretary shall call alphabetically the roll of the members entitled to vote, and as each one's name is called, he shall deposit his ballot; but no member is entitled to a vote, nor can he be elected to any office, who is not clear in the books of the Lodge. A majority of all the votes cast shall be necessary to a choice.

SEC. 4. No member can be elected as Worshipful Master who has not been duly elected, and served as a Warden

SEC. 5. The installation of Officers shall take place as soon as practicable after their election, but it shall be before or on St. John's Day in December of each year.

ARTICLE V.

Duties of Officers.

SECTION 1. The Treasurer shall receive all moneys from the Secretary; shall keep an accurate and just account thereof; shall pay the same out only upon an order duly signed by the Master and countersigned by the Secretary. He shall, at the regular meetings in June and December (preceding St. John's Day), of each year, submit a report in full of the monetary transactions of the Lodge. The Lodge may also at any time, when considered necessary, cause him to present an account of his receipts and disbursements, and of the amount of funds on hand.

SEC. 2. He shall, if required by the Lodge, execute a good and sufficient bond to the Master for the faithful performance of his duties.

SEC. 3. The Secretary shall keep a faithful record of all proceedings proper to be written; shall transmit a copy of the same to the Grand Lodge when required; shall keep a separate account for each member of the Lodge; shall report at the regular meetings in June and December (preceding St. John's Day), the amounts due by each; shall receive all moneys due the Lodge, and pay the same to the Treasurer; shall forthwith notify the Grand Secretary of all rejections, suspensions and expulsions in the Lodge, and shall perform all such other duties as may properly appertain to his office.

SEC. 4. He shall receive such compensation for his services as the Lodge may direct.

SEC. 5. The Tyler in addition to the necessary duties of his office, shall serve all notices and summonses, and perform such other services as may be required of him by the Lodge.

SEC. 6. He shall receive such compensation for his services as the Lodge may direct.

SEC. 7. The Trustees of the Lodge shall hold and take title to, and invest all funds of the Lodge as Trustees of——— No.———, they shall collect all interest due the Lodge and pay the same over to the Secretary, and they shall examine the books, vouchers, etc., of the Treasurer and Secretary. All their operations shall be subject to the revision of the Lodge, and they shall report in writing all their doings, at the regular meetings preceding St. John's Day, in June and December of each year.

SEC. 8. They shall, if required by the Lodge, execute a good and sufficient bond to the Worshipful Master for the faithful performance of their duties.

10

ARTICLE VI.

Revenues.

SECTION 1. The table of fees for this Lodge shall be as follows: For the Degree of Entered Apprentice, $———; for the degree of Fellow Craft, $———; for the degree of Master Mason, $———. The fee for each degree must always accompany the petition.

SEC. 2. The dues of each member of the Lodge shall be $——— per annum, payable quarterly in advance.

ARTICLE VII.

Committees.

SECTION 1. There shall be three standing Committees of the Lodge, who shall be appointed by the Worshipful Master immediately after his installation, viz: A Committee on Charity; a Committee on Grievance; an Auditing Committee.

SEC. 2. The Committee on Charity shall consist of the Worshipful Master and Wardens, and shall have the power to draw upon the Treasurer any sum not exceeding $——— at any one time, for the relief of a distressed worthy Brother, his wife, widow or orphans.

SEC. 3. The Committee on Grievance shall consist of three members of the Lodge, of which the Senior Warden shall be Chairman, to whom all differences between Brethren shall be referred. It shall be the duty of said Committee to reconcile Brethren to each other, if ill feeling exist, as soon as the same shall come to their knowledge.

SEC. 4. The Auditing Committee shall consist of three members, of which the Junior Warden shall be Chairman, whose duty it shall be to examine and audit all claims presented against the Lodge.

ARTICLE VIII.

Trial and Punishment.

SECTION 1. The Trial Code, adopted by the Most Worshipful Grand Lodge of Utah, November 12th, A. D. 1874, is adopted by this Lodge and shall be published with these By-Laws.

ARTICLE IX.

Miscellaneous.

SECTION 1. Any member in good standing, whose dues are paid, and against whom no charges are pending, may withdraw from this Lodge at any time by giving notice of his intention so to do at a regular meeting, when he shall be entitled to a dimit in the usual form.

SEC. 2. Any member of this Lodge being twelve months in arrears for dues and residing within the jurisdiction of the Grand Lodge of Utah, shall be notified by the Secretary that unless within thirty days, or if residing without the jurisdiction of the Grand Lodge, within sixty days from the date of the regular meeting at which such delinquency shall be made known to the Lodge, either his dues

be paid, or sickness or inability to pay be shown as the cause of such refusal or neglect, he will be liable to suspension from all the rights and privileges of Masonry. If neither of the foregoing excuses be made, he may at the first regular meeting after the expiration of the specified time, be declared by the Master to be suspended, unless for special reasons shown, the Lodge shall remit his dues or grant him further time for payment. But any member thus suspended, who shall at any time pay the arrearages due at the time of his suspension, or who shall have such arrearages remitted by the Lodge, shall be declared by the Master thereof restored.

Sec. 3. Any member refusing obedience to a Lodge summons shall be subject to Masonic discipline.

Sec. 4. When a candidate for affiliation is rejected, or a Brother reprimanded, suspended or expelled, no member or visitor shall reveal, either directly or indirectly, to such person or to any other, any transactions which may have taken place on the subject; nor shall any proceeding of the Lodge, not proper to be made public, be disclosed outside thereof, under the penalty of reprimand, suspension or expulsion, as the Lodge may determine.

Sec. 5. No member of this Lodge present and entitled to a vote, shall be excused from that duty, save by unanimous consent of the Lodge.

Sec. 6. All reports of Committees must be reduced to writing. The first named Brother on each Committee is Chairman of the same.

Sec. 7. Non-Affiliated Masons shall not be allowed to visit this Lodge more than six months without paying regular dues, nor shall any non-Affiliated Mason be entitled to any of the privileges of contributing members.*

ARTICLE X.

Rules of Order.

Section 1. The regular order of business at every regular meeting of this Lodge shall be as follows:

1. Reading of the minutes.
2. Reports of Committees on Investigation.
3. Ballotings.
4. Reception of petitions.
5. Miscellaneous and Unfinished Business.
6. Conferring Degrees.

ARTICLE XI.

Amendments.

Section 1. Any alteration or amendment to these By-Laws shall be proposed in writing, at a regular meeting of the Lodge, and lie over until next regular meeting, when, by a vote of two-thirds of the members present, such alterations or amendments may be adopted; but such amendment shall have no effect until approved by the Grand Lodge or the Grand Master of Utah

---

*See Standing Resolution No. 11.

The Ancient Charges of a Freemason.

A. D. 1717.

EXTRACTED FROM THE ANCIENT RECORDS OF LODGES THROUGHOUT THE WORLD.

CHARGE I.

Concerning God and Religion.

A Mason is obliged, by his tenure, to obey the moral law; and if he rightly understand the art, he will never be a stupid atheist nor an irreligious libertine. He, of all men, should best understand that God seeth not as man seeth; for man looketh at the outward appearance, but God looketh to the heart. A Mason is, therefore, particularly bound never to act against the dictates of his conscience. Let a man's religion, or mode of worship, be what it may, he is not excluded from the Fraternity, provided he believe in the glorious Architect of heaven and earth, and practice the sacred duties of morality. Masons unite with the virtuous of every persuasion in the firm and pleasing bond of fraternal love, they are taught to view the errors of mankind with compassion, and to strive, by the purity of their own conduct, to demonstrate the superior excellence of the faith they may profess. Thus Masonry is the centre of union between good men and true, and the happy means of conciliating friendship among those who must otherwise have remained at a perpetual distance.

CHARGE II.

Of the Civil Magistrate.

A Mason is a peaceful subject to the civil powers wherever he resides or or works, and is never to be concerned in plots and conspiracies against the peace and welfare of the nation, nor to behave himself undutifully to inferior magistrates. He is cheerfully to conform to every lawful authority; to uphold on every occasion, the interests of the community; and zealously promote the prosperity of his own country. Masonry has ever flourished in times of peace and been always injured by war, bloodshed and confusion; so that kings and princes, in every age have been much disposed to encourage the craftsmen on account of their peaceableness and loyalty, whereby they practically answer the cavils of their adversaries and promote the honor of the Fraternity. Craftsmen are bound by peculiar ties to promote peace, cultivate harmony, and live in concord and brotherly love

CHARGE III.

Of Lodges.

A Lodge is a place where Freemasons assemble to work and to instruct and improve themselves in the mysteries of their ancient science. In an extended sense it applies to persons as well as to place; hence every regular assembly or duly organized meeting of Masons is called a Lodge. Every Brother ought to belong to some Lodge and be subject to its By-Laws and the general regulations of the Craft. A Lodge may be either general or particular, as will be best understood by attending it, and there a knowledge of the established usages and customs of the Craft is alone to be acquired. From ancient times no Master or Fellow could be absent from his Lodge, especially when warned to appear at it, without incurring a severe censure, unless it appeared to the Master and Wardens that pure necessity hindered him.

The persons made Masons or admitted members of a Lodge must be good and true men, free-born, and of mature and discreet age and sound judgment, no bondmen, no women, no immoral and scandalous men, but of good report.

CHARGE IV.

Of Masters, Wardens, Fellows and Apprentices.

All preferment among Masons is grounded upon real worth and personal merit only, that so the Lord's may be well served, the Brethren not put to shame, nor the Royal Craft despised; therefore no Master or Warden is chosen by seniority but for his merit. It is impossible to describe these things in writing, and therefore every Brother must attend in his place, and learn them in a way peculiar to this Fraternity. Candidates may, nevertheless, know that no Master should take an Apprentice, unless he has sufficient employment for him; and, unless he be a *perfect youth, having no maim or defect in his body,* that may render him incapable of learning the art, of serving his Master's Lord, and of being made a Brother, and then a Fellow-Craft in due time, after he has served such a term of years as the custom of the country directs; and that he should be descended of honest parents, that so, when otherwise qualified, he may arrive at the honor of being the Warden and then the Master of the Lodge, the Grand Warden, and at length the Grand Master of all the Lodges, according to his merit.

No Brother can be a Warden until he has passed the part of a Fellow-Craft, nor a Master until he has acted as a Warden, nor Grand Warden until he has been Master of a Lodge, nor Grand Master until he has been a Fellow-Craft before his election, who is also to be nobly born, or a gentleman of the best fashion, or some eminent scholar, or some curious architect, or other artist descended of honest parents, and who is of singularly great merit in the opinion of the Lodges.

11

The rulers and governors, supreme and subordinate, of the Ancient Lodge, are to be obeyed in their respective stations by all the Brethren, according to the old Charges and Regulations, with all humility, reverence, love and alacrity.

N. B.—In ancient times, no Brother, however skilled in the Craft, was called a Master Mason until he had been elected into the chair of a Lodge.

CHARGE V.

Of the Management of the Craft in Working.

All Masons shall work honestly on working days that they may live creditably on holy days; and the time appointed by the law of the land, or confirmed by custom, shall be observed.

The most expert of the Fellow Craftsmen shall be chosen or appointed the Master, or overseer of the Lord's work, who is to be called Master by those who work under him. The Craftsmen are to avoid all ill language, and to call each other by no disobliging name, but Brother or Fellow, and to behave themselves courteously within and without the Lodge.

The Master, knowing himself to be able of cunning, shall undertake the Lord's work as reasonably as possible, and truly dispend his goods as if they were his own; nor to give more wages to any Brother or Apprentice than he may really deserve.

Both the Master and the Masons receiving their wages justly, shall be faithful to the Lord, and honestly finish their work, whether task or journey, nor put the work to task that hath been accustomed to journey.

None shall discover envy at the prosperity of a Brother, nor supplant him, or put him out of his work, if he be capable to finish the same, for no man can finish another's work so much to the Lord's profit, unless he be thoroughly acquainted with the designs and draughts of him that began it.

When a Fellow-Craftsman is chosen Warden of the work under the Master, he shall be true both to the Master and Fellows, shall carefully oversee the work in the Master's absence, to the Lord's profit, and his Brethren shall obey him.

All Masons employed shall meekly receive their wages without murmuring or mutiny, and not desert the Master till the work be finished.

A younger Brother shall be instructed in working to prevent spoiling the materials for want of judgment, and for increasing and continuing of brotherly love.

All the tools used in working shall be approved by the Grand Lodge.

No laborer shall be employed in the proper work of Masonry, nor shall Freemasons work with those that are not free, without an urgent necessity; nor shall they teach laborers and unaccepted Masons, as they should teach a Brother or Fellow.

CHARGE VI.

Of Behavior, viz: 1—In the Lodge while Constituted.

You are not to hold private Committees or separate conversation, without leave from the Master, nor to talk of anything impertinently or unseemly, nor interrupt the Master or Wardens, or any Brother **speaking to** the Master, nor behave yourself ludicrously or jestingly while the **Lodge** is engaged in what is serious and solemn; nor use any unbecoming language upon any pretense whatsoever, **but** to pay due reverence to your Master, Wardens and Fellows, and put them to Worship.

If any **complaint be brought,** the Brother found **guilty shall stand to the** award and determination of the Lodge, who are the proper and competent judges of all such controversies (unless you carry them by appeal to the Grand **Lodge),** and to whom **they** ought to be **referred,** unless a Lord's work be **hindered the** meanwhile, **in which** case a particular reference may **be made; but you must** never go to law about what concerneth **Masonry,** without an absolute **necessity** apparent to the Lodge.

2—Behavior after the Lodge is **over and the** *Brethren not* **Gone.**

You may enjoy yourselves **with innocent** mirth, treating **one** another according to ability, but avoiding all excess, **or** forcing any Brother to eat or drink beyond his inclination, **or** hindering him from going when his occasions call him, or doing or saying **anything** offensive, or that may forbid an easy and free conversation, for that **would blast our** harmony and defeat our laudable purposes. Therefore no **private piques or** quarrels must be brought within the door of the **Lodge,** far **less any** quarrels about religion or nations or State policy, we being **only as** Masons **of the** universal religion above mentioned, we are also of all **nations,** tongues, kindreds and languages, and **are resolved against all politics, as** what **never yet** conduced to the welfare of the **Lodge nor ever will.**

3—Behavior when Brethren Meet without Strangers, but not in a Lodge Formed.

You are to salute one another in a courteous manner, as you will be instructed, calling each other Brother, freely giving mutual instructoin as shall be thought expedient, without being overseen or overheard, and without encroaching upon each other or derogating from that respect **which is** due to any Brother, were he not a Mason, for though all Masons are **as** Brethren upon the same level, yet Masonry takes no honor from **a** man that he had before; nay, rather it adds to his honor, especially if he has deserved well of the Brotherhood, who must give honor to whom it is due and avoid ill manners.

4—Behavior in Presence of Strangers not Masons.

You should be cautious in your words and carriage, that the most penetrating **stranger shall** not be able to discover or find out what is not proper to be intimated**;** and sometimes **you shall divert** a discourse, and manage it prudently for the honor of the worshipful Fraternity.

5—Behavior at Home and in Your Neighborhood.

You are to act as becomes a moral and wise man, particularly not to **let your** family, **friends** and neighbors know the concerns of the **Lodge, etc., but wisely**

to consult your own honor, and that of your Ancient Brotherhood, for reasons not to be mentioned here. You must also consult your health by not continuing together too late or too long from home after Lodge hours are past, and by avoiding of gluttony or drunkenness, that your families be not neglected or injured nor you disabled from working.

6—*Behavior toward a Strange Brother.*

You are cautiously to examine him in such a method as prudence shall direct you, that you may not be imposed upon by an ignorant, false pretender, whom you are to reject with contempt and derision, and beware of giving him any hints of knowledge.

But if you discover him to be a true and genuine Brother, you are to respect him accordingly, and if he is in want you must relieve him if you can, or else direct him how he may be relieved. You must employ him some days or else recommend him to be employed. But you are not charged to do beyond your ability, only to prefer a poor Brother that is a good man and true, before any other people in the same circumstances.

Finally, all these charges you are to observe, and also those that shall be communicated to you in another way, cultivating brotherly love, the foundation and cap-stone, the cement and glory of this Ancient Fraternity, avoiding all wrangling and quarreling, all slander and backbiting, nor permitting others to slander any honest Brother but defending his character and doing him all good offices, as far as is consistent with your honor and safety and no farther.   And if any of them do you injury, you must apply to your own or his Lodge and from thence you may appeal to the Grand Lodge at the Annual Communication, as has been the ancient, laudable conduct of our forefathers in every nation; never taking a legal course but when the case cannot be otherwise decided, and patiently listen to the honest and friendly advice of Master and Fellows, when they would prevent your going to law with strangers or would advise you to put a speedy period to all lawsuits, that so you may find the affair of Masonry with the more alacrity and success; but with respect to Brothers or Fellows at law, the Master and Brethren should kindly offer their mediation, which ought to be thankfully submitted to by the contending Brethren; and if that submission is impracticable, they must, however, carry on their process or lawsuit, without wrath or rancor (not in the common way), saying or doing nothing which may hinder brotherly love and good offices to be renewed and continued, that all may see the benign influence of Masonry, as all true Masons have done from the beginning of the world and will do to the end of time.

AMEN, *so mote it be.*

ANCIENT LANDMARKS.

(From Bro. John W. Simons' "Principles of Masonic Jurisprudence.")

1. A belief in the existence of a Supreme Being, and in the immortality of the soul.

2. That the moral law, which inculcates, among other things, charity and probity, industry and sobriety, is the rule and guide of every Mason.

3. Respect for, and obedience to the civil law of the country, and the Masonic Regulations of the jurisdiction where a Mason may reside.

4. That new-made Masons must be free-born, of lawful age and hale and sound at the time of making.

5. The modes of recognition, and generally the rites and ceremonies of the three Degrees of Ancient Craft Masonry.

6. That no appeal can be taken to the Lodge, from the decision of the Master, or the Warden occupying the Chair in his absence.

7. That no one can be the Master of a warranted Lodge till he has been installed, and served one year as Warden.

8. That when a man becomes a Mason, he not only acquires membership in the particular Lodge that admits him, but in a general sense he becomes one of the whole Masonic Family, and hence he has a right to visit Masonically every regular Lodge, except when such visit is likely to disturb the harmony or interrupt the working of the Lodge he proposes to visit.

9. The prerogative of the Grand Master to preside over every assembly of the Craft within his jurisdiction, to make Masons at sight in a regular Lodge and to grant Dispensations for the formation of new Lodges.

10. That no one can be made a Mason, save in a regular Lodge, duly convened, after petition, and acceptance by unanimous ballot, except when made at sight by the Grand Master.

11. That the ballot for candidates is strictly and inviolably secret.

12. That a Lodge cannot try its Master.

13. That every Mason is amenable to the Laws and Regulations of the jurisdiction in which he resides, even though he be a member of a particular Lodge in some other jurisdiction.

14. The right of the Craft at large to be represented in Grand Lodge, and to instruct their representatives.

15. The general aim and form of the society, as handed down to us by the fathers, to be by us preserved inviolate and transmitted to our successors forever.

Form of Records for Constituent Lodges.

(Notes: Head with "Regular" or "Special" Meeting, as the case may be.—Lodge Meetings are in the Standard By-Laws called "Meetings," those of the Grand Lodge "Communications."

The Grand Master opens a Lodge in *ample form*, his Deputy in *due form*, a Worshipful Master in *form*.

If during the Meeting the Grand Master or an elective Grand or an elective Past Grand Officer from a sister Grand Jurisdiction, or a distinguished Mason from abroad visits the Lodge, state the particulars of his reception and the addresses delivered on the occasion, &c.)

HALL OF AURUM LODGE, No. 50, A. F. & A. M.

Argenta,————, A. D. 18—.

Regular meeting.

PRESENT:

Bro. A. B., Worshipful Master; Bro. N. O., Marshal;

Bro. C. D., Senior Warden; Bro. P. Q., Senior Deacon;

Bro. E. F., Junior Warden; Bro. R. S., Junior Deacon;

Bro. G. H., Treasurer; Bro. T. U., Senior Steward;

Bro. I. K., Secretary; Bro. V. W., Junior Steward;

Bro. L. M., Chaplain; Bro. X. Y., Tyler.

Members and visiting Brethren as per Tyler's Register.

The Lodge opened at 8 o'clock, P. M., in the Master Mason's Degree in *Form*.

Minutes, read, approved and signed.
The minutes of the last regular meeting, held————, and subsequent intervening meetings, held————, and————, were read by the Secretary, and being found correct, were approved and signed by the Worshipful Master. (If corrected by the Master or any member, state it.)

Report of Investigating Committees.
The Investigating Committees on the petitions of Mr. A. B. for the three Degrees, and of Bro. C. D. for affiliation, each severally, reported favorable.

The Investigating Committee on the petition of Mr. E. F. reported not favorable.

The reports were severally received and the Committees discharged.

The ballots were then spread separately on the petition of Bro. C. D. for affiliation and of Messrs. A. B. and E. F. for the degrees. *Ballots.—Bro. C. D. and Mr. A. B. elected. Mr. E. F. rejected.*

Bro. C. D. and Mr. A. B. were declared duly elected and Mr. E. F. rejected.

The Worshipful Master instructed the Secretary to notify the Grand Secretary of the above rejection, and to inform Mr. E. F. of the action of the Lodge and return to him the initiation fee. *To notify Grand Secretary and return fees.*

A petition for affiliation, recommended by Bros. A. B. and C. D. was received from Bro. E. F. On motion the petition was received and referred to Bros. G. H., I. K, and L. M. for investigation. *Reception of Petitions, Bro. E. F. for affiliation.*

A petition for the three Degrees, recommended by Bros. N. O. and P. Q., accompanied with the initiation fee of fifty dollars, was received from Mr. R. S. On motion the petition was received and referred to Bros. T. U., V. W. and X. Y. for investigation. *Mr. R. S. for the three degrees.*

The Secretary read an official communication from the Most Worshipful A. B., Grand Master of Masons in Utah, in words as follows:——(Copy communication.) *Miscellaneous and Unfinished Business. Communication from Grand Master.*

(All official communications emanating from the Grand Lodge or the Grand Master must be spread on the minutes in full, also the action of the Lodge thereon.)

The Secretary then read the quarterly report of the Grand Secretary, and was instructed to spread the names of those rejected, etc. during the past quarter, in the "Black Book," and file the communication in the archives of the Lodge. *Quarterly Report of Grand Secretary read.*

Bro. C. D., elected this evening, entered the Lodge, was welcomed by the Worshipful Master and signed the By-Laws as a member. *Bro. C. D. signs By-Laws.*

A bill from Messrs. John Doe & Co., to the amount of $11.50, for stationery, having been examined by the Auditing Committee and found correct, was, on motion, ordered paid. (Here insert all other reports from regular or special Committees.) *Stationery $11.50.*

Bro. X. Y. presented his monthly bill as Tyler of this Lodge, amounting to $17, which was, on motion, referred to the Auditing Committee for examination and approval. (Here insert all other bills presented and state how they were disposed of.) *Tyler's bill referred to Auditing Committee.*

Bro. A. B. offered the following amendment to section—of Art. —, of the By-Laws, which the Worshipful Master ordered to be spread on the minutes in full, and in accordance with Sec. 1 of Art. XI to lay over till the next regular meeting. (Here copy the amendment.) *Amendment to By-Laws.*

Resolution offered relative to.

The following resolution was offered by Bro. C. D. (Copy resolution in full.)

After some time spent in consideration of the reslution, the whole subject was, on motion, laid on the table until the next regular meeting (or such other action as was really had.)

Charges preferred against Bro. L. M.

Bro. E. F., Junior Warden, presented the following charges and specifications: (Copy charges and specifications in full.)

Order given to summon members.

The Worshipful Master ordered the Secretary to issue summonses for all members residing in this city to be present at the next regular meeting, for the purpose of electing six Commissioners to try the charges in accordance with the Trial Code of our Grand Jurisdiction.

Hall Committee report adopted.

The report of the Hall Commitee laid on the table at the last regular meeting was taken up, and after a full discussion, on motion, adopted.

The amendment to Sect. —Art. — of By-Laws adopted.

The amendment to Sec.— of Art.—of the By-Laws of this Lodge as offered by Bro. L. M. at the regular meeting was taken up, and thoroughly discussed. The vote being counted and twenty-one out of thirty members present having voted in the affirmative, the Worshipful Master declared the amendment adopted as a part of the By-Laws of this Lodge. The Secretary was instructed to transmit a copy of the amendment to the Grand Secretary for the approval of the Most Worshipful Grand Master. (Note: All amendments to By-Laws must be approved by the Grand Lodge or Grand Master before they become law and the approval must appear in the minutes.)

(Under the head of "Miscellaneous and Unfinished Busiuess" many other matters may come before the Lodge, all of which should here be inserted.)

By order of the Worshipful Master labor in the Master Mason's Degree was suspended, and a Lodge of Fellow-Craft Masons opened in lieu thereof. Bro. L. M. was then examined as to his proficiency in this Degree after which the Lodge closed in the Fellow-Craft Degree and resumed labor in the Master Mason's Degree.

Bro. L. M. examined.

Bro. L. M. raised.

The Lodge being satisfied with the examination, and Bro. L. M. being in attendance, he was duly prepared, introduced and raised to the Degree of a Master Mason, according to the ancient custom, received the lectures and charges thereto belonging, signed the By-Laws of the Lodge and was welcomed by the Worshipful Master as a member thereof.

The following are the receipts since the last regular meeting and of this evening:

Trustees' interest,......................	$17 50
Bro. L. M., Master Mason's Degree,......... ...	10
Bro. A. B., dues,.......................	6
Bro. C. D., dues,.......................	12
Mr. R. S., Initiation fee..................	50

Total, ... $95 50

Which sum was paid to the Treasurer and his receipt taken.

There being no further business, the Lodge closed at 10 o'clock P. M., in *form*; peace and harmony prevailing.

A. B., *Worshipful Master*.

I. K., *Secretary*.

(NOTES: When a special meeting is called for the purpose of conferring Degrees, the Master should, after opening the Lodge, state the object of the meeting, and the following rules should be observed and accordingly entered by the Secretary in the minutes of the evening:

The vote on the proficiency is taken in the Degree the candidate is about to receive, in all other matters the Secretary may be guided by the instruction given for raising in regular meeting.)

When called for the purpose of conferring the Entered Apprentice Degree, the Lodge will be opened, do the work and close in that Degree.

When a Lodge is called for the purpose of conferring the Fellow-Craft Degree, it shall be opened in that Degree, suspend labor and open in the Entered Apprentice Degree for examination, when concluded, close in that Degree, resume labor in the Fellow-Craft Degree, do the work, and close in that Degree.

When a Lodge is called for the purpose of conferring the Master Mason's Degree, it shall be opened in that Degree, suspend labor and open in the Fellow-Craft Degree for examination, when concluded close in that Degree, resume labor in the Master Mason's Degree, do the work, and close in that Degree.

13

FORM OF TRIAL RECORDS FOR CONSTITUENT LODGES.

ABSTRACT OF THE RECORDS OF THE TRIAL OF JOHN DOE FOR UN-MASONIC (OR GROSS UN-MASONIC) CONDUCT.

HALL OF AURUM LODGE, No. 50, A. F. AND A. M., }
ARGENTA, A. D. 18—. }

AURUM LODGE, No. 50, A. F. & A. M. }
vs. }
JOHN DOE. }

At a regular meeting of Aurum Lodge, No. 50, held at its Hall, in the city of Argenta, March 3d, 1879, the following charges were presented, viz:

(Here insert the exact copy of the charges and specifications commencing with, "A true copy—").

The Worshipful Master ordered the charge and specifications spread on the minutes in full and instructed the Secretary to issue summonses for the members of the Lodge, residing in this city, to be in attendance at the next regular meeting.

The following is a true copy of that portion of the minutes of a regular meeting of Aurum Lodge, No. 50, held April 4th, 1879, referring to the arraignment of Bro. John Doe.

"The Worshipful Master ordered the names of members present to be called and recorded.—There were twenty-seven in attendance.—He then directed the Secretary to read the charge and specifications against Bro. John Doe, and after reading Rule 1 of Section 2, of the Trial Code, ordered an election for six Commissioners with the following result: Bros. A. B., C. D., E. F., G. H., I. J. and K. L."

The Worshipful Master instructed the Secretary to present a certified copy of the charge and specifications to the accused (if his place of residence is unknown, a copy of the charge and specifications should be sent to his last known Post Office address), and to notify him and all other parties interested in the trial, that the trial would be held in our Hall, on the 6th day of May, A. D. 1879, at 7:30 o'clock, P. M.

(If the Worshipful Master should appoint a counsel for the accused or an assistant to the prosecuting Officer, insert it here.)

THE TRIAL.

Hall of Aurum Lodge, No. 50, A. F. & A. M. }
Argenta, May 6th, 1879. }

The Commissioners elected at a regular meeting of Aurum Lodge, No. 50, held April 4th, to try the charges against Bro. John Doe assembled this day, at 7:30 o'clock P. M.

The Worshipful Master ordered the roll to be called, and the following Brethren were found present: Bro. M. N., Worshipful Master; Bro. O. P., Secretary; Bro. Q. R., Junior Warden, *as Prosecuting Attorney;* Bro. John Doe, *Defendant;* Bro. S. T., *Counsel for the Defense;* Bros. A. B.; C. D.; E. F.; G. H.; I. J.; K. L.; *Commissioners.*

(If the defendant is not present, and the trial held *ex parte,* it should be here stated, and in that case, the first witness, after calling the meeting to order, should be the Secretary, who should testify that he had forwarded a copy of the charges and notice of time of trial to the last known Post Office address of Bro. John Doe; and that the document had been returned by the Postmaster, or any other facts.)

The Worshipful Master called the meeting to order and directed the Secretary to read the charges.

The accused pleaded not guilty (or guilty, as the case may be.)

Bro. Q. R., Junior Warden, introduced as witnesses, Messrs. U. V. and W. X., who, before giving their testimony were sworn before Mr. Y. Z., a Notary Public, of the county of———, Territory of Utah.

The next witness, Bro. B. A. testified on his honor as a Master Mason, as follows:

(All evidence, as taken down, by questions and answers, should be given as near as possible in full.)

(If cross-examined by counsel for defense, or any other party interested in the trial, insert it here.)

The prosecution then rested, and Bro. B. C. testified for the defense as follows: (Insert evidence as above.)

The examination of witnesses here closed and the case was referred to the Commissioners with (or without) argument by either counsel. (State main points of arguments, if made.)

The Worshipful Master called the attention of the Commissioners to the Trial Code, and read Rule 7 of Section 2, and all retired, save the Commissioners.

The following is a true copy of that portion of the Records of Aurum Lodge, No. 50, referring to the arraignment of John Doe, held at its Hall, June 7th, 1879.

The Worshipful Master opened the envelope containing the findings of the Commissioners in the case of Aurum Lodge, No. 50, A. F. & A. M., vs. John Doe, and ordered the Secretary to read the same, which is as follows:

A true copy:

"HALL OF AURUM LODGE, No. 50, A. F. &A. M., }
Argenta, June 7th, A. D. 1879. }

To the Worshipful Master, Wardens and Members of Aurum Lodge, No. 50, A. F. & A. M.:

SIRS AND BROTHERS: We, the undersigned Commissioners, elected at a regular meeting of this Lodge, held April 4th, A. D. 1879, to try the charges against Bro. John Doe, for gross un-Masonic conduct, beg leave to report, that we have complied with the duties assigned us, and after due trial and full consideration of the evidence submitted and action on our part as prescribed in Rule 7, of Section 2, of the Trial Code, we do find the said Bro. John Doe, guilty of the offense he is charged with, and have voted that he be expelled from all the rights and privileges of Freemasonry (or reprimanded or suspended for a definite or indefinite period, as the case may be).

[Signed.]   Here follow the names of the six Commissioners.

The Worshipful Master ordered the Secretary to spread the findings of the Commissioners in full, in the minutes of this meeting, and record it as the judgment of the Lodge."

Bro. John Doe being present, the Worshipful Master pronounced him expelled, whereupon he notified the Lodge that he would appeal to the Most Worshipful Grand Lodge of Utah, at its next Annual Communication.

A true copy of the Appeal.

"*To the Worshipful Master of Aurum Lodge, No. 50, A. F. & A. M.:*

DEAR SIR AND WORSHIPFUL BROTHER: Take notice, that I intend to appeal from the action (or decision), of your Lodge, in the matter of the charges preferred against me by Bro. Q. R., Junior Warden, whereby I was convicted of said charges and sentence of expulsion passed against me (or set forth any other decision from which appeal is taken), and you are hereby requested to make out and forward to the Grand Secretary of the Most Worshipful Grand Lodge of Utah, certified copies of all papers, proofs, records and proceedings pertaining to said matter, preparatory to the trial of said appeal at the next Annual Communication, of the said Grand Lodge of Utah.

Dated, Argenta, June 7th, 1879.   JOHN DOE.

NOTE:—A copy of the Appeal to Grand Lodge must also accompany the Abstract.

I, O. P., Secretary of Aurum Lodge, No. 50, A. F. & A. M., do hereby certify that the foregoing contains a true and full transcript of the proceedings of said Lodge, in the trial of Aurum Lodge, No. 50, A. F. & A M., vs. John Doe.

IN TESTIMONY WHEREOF, I have hereunto set my hand and affixed the Seal of our Lodge, this the ——day of ——, A. D. 1879.

{ SEAL }

O. P., *Secretary.*"

NOTE. The above form may have to be altered in many instances, but nevertheless may be considered a guide for Secretaries in preparing and making out transcripts of trial records.

FORM OF CHARGES FOR CONSTITUENT LODGES.

———

To the Worshipful Master, Wardens and Brethren of **Aurum** *Lodge, No.* 50, *Ancient, Free and* **Accepted Masons:**

Bro. John **Doe**, a Master Mason (or F. C. or E. A.), of (here state the residence, membership, affiliation, non-affiliation or other Masonic standing of the accused), is hereby charged with un-Masonic (or gross un-Masonic), conduct in this, to wit:

SPECIFICATION 1:—That the said John Doe on the ——day of——, A. D. 18—, at the town (village or city) of——, in the county of——, Utah, did violently assault and strike Bro. A. B.

SPECIFICATION 2:—That the said John **Doe**, on the day and at the place aforesaid, did speak and use toward the said **Bro. A. B.** the following **scandalous** and insulting language, to wit: (Here set **out the words** used.)

SPECIFICATION 3:—That the said John Doe, on the day and at the place aforesaid, did, in presence and hearing of several persons, speak and **utter, of and** concerning the said Bro. A. B., the following slanderous and malicious words, to wit: (Here set out the words.)

All of which acts of the said John Doe were in violation of his duties and obligations as a Mason, and to the injury of the said A. B., as well as to the scandal and disgrace of the Masonic Fraternity; wherefore it is demanded that the said John Doe be put upon trial therefor, and dealt with according to Masonic law and usage.

Dated, ——, A. D. 18—,   C. D. *Junior Warden.*

(It is made the especial duty of the Junior Warden, in the absence of other accusers, to prefer all charges for offenses committed when the Lodge is not at labor; but the neglect or refusal of the Junior Warden to perform such duty shall not prevent any other Brother from preferring and prosecuting any charge of un-Masonic conduct which may come to his knowledge.)

(All names should be written in full, if known. Specifications should be added for each separate state of facts constituting a Masonic offense, with reasonable certainty as to time, place and other particulars.)

14

FORM OF SPECIFICATION FOR DRUNKENNESS.

1. That the said John Doe, on the——day of——, A. D. 18—, at ——, in the county of——, Utah, was in a state of gross intoxication, from the intemperate use of intoxicating and spirituous liquors.

2. That the said John Doe, on the——day of——, A. D. 18—, at ——, in the county of———, Utah, and for a long time previous thereto, to wit: for——years last past, and at divers other places in the said county and Territory, and notwithstanding the frequent warnings and admonitions of the Officers and Brethren of this Lodge—was addicted to the excessive use of intoxicating liquors, and to the evil habit of frequent and gross intoxication and drunkenness.

FORM OF SPECIFICATION FOR THEFT.

That the said John Doe, on the——day of——, A. D. 18—, at ——, in the county of———, Utah. did wilfully steal and take from Bro. A. B. (or Mr. A. B.) of————, twenty dollars in money. (If the theft be of other property than money describe the property.)

FORM OF SPECIFICATION FOR FRAUD.

That the said John Doe, on the——day of——, A. D. 18—, at——, in the county of———, Utah did wilfully cheat, wrong and defraud Bro. A. B., by making to said A. B. certain false and fraudulent representations concerning a certain horse which he then and there sold to the said A. B., and which the said A. B. was by means of said false representations then and there induced to buy and to pay therefor a large sum of money, to wit: the sum of one hundred dollars; which represenoptions were, that the said horse was sound, true and kind, when in fact the said horse was not such, as the said John Doe well knew.

FORM OF SUMMONS, TO BE ACCOMPANIED WITH A COPY OF THE CHARGES AND SPECIFICATIONS.

To Bro. John Doe, of——:

You are hereby summoned and required to appear at a meeting of the Com- missioners of Aurum Lodge, No. 50, Ancient, Free and Accepted Masons, to be held at its Hall at——, in the county of———, Utah, on the——day of———, A. D. 18—, at—o'clock—, then and there to make answer to charges and specifi- cations now on file against you in said Lodge, a true copy of which charges and specifications is hereto annexed.

Dated——, A. D. 18—.

By order of the Worshipful Master,
E. F., Secretary.

FORM OF APPEAL TO GRAND LODGE.

To the M∴ W∴ Grand Lodge of Ancient, Free and Accepted Masons of Utah:

The undersigned hereby appeals to your Most Worshipful Body from the decision of Aurum Lodge, No. 50, of Ancient, Free and Accepted Masons, in the matter of certain charges and specifications preferred in said Lodge against this appellant, by C. D., Junior Warden, whereby this appellant was convicted of the said charges and specifications, and sentence of expulsion passed against him; and he specifies the following as the ground of his appeal, viz:

(Here state grounds.)

All of which will more fully appear from the records, proofs and proceedings in the case.   JOHN DOE, *Appellant.*

Dated, —— —, A. D. 18—,

(NOTE: For Form of Appeal to Lodge see page 52.

Blank Forms for Constituent Lodges.

FORM OF CERTIFICATE FOR A DIPLOMA.

———Lodge No.—, A. F. and A. M.,
———————————, A. D. 18— }

To the Right Worshipful———, *Grand Secretary of the Grand Lodge of Utah:*

I hereby certify that Bro.———is a Master Mason and a member of this Lodge, in good standing; and as such he is recommended for a Grand Lodge Diploma, upon payment of the usual fees.

Given under my hand and the Seal of the Lodge aforesaid, at the date above written.

[SEAL.]

——— ———, *Secretary,*

FORM OF CERTIFICATE FOR A DIPLOMA FOR THE BENEFIT OF THE FAMILY OF A DECEASED BROTHER.

Lodge, No.—, A. F. and A. M. }
———————————, A. D. 18—. }

To the Right Worshipful———, *Grand Secretary of the Grand Lodge of Utah:*

I hereby certify that Bro.———, who died at———, on the———day of——— A. D. 18—, was, at the date of his decease, a Master Mason and a member of this Lodge, in good standing; and that he left (here insert a widow, a child or children, or any of them, as the case may be), for whose benefit a Grand Lodge Diploma is desired.

Given by order of the Lodge aforesaid, at the date first above written, as witness my hand and the Seal thereof.

[SEAL.]

———————, *Secretary.*

FORM OF PETITION FOR A DISPENSATION TO FORM A NEW LODGE.

To the Most Worshipful Grand Master of Masons in Utah:

The petition of the undersigned respectfully represents, that they are Master Masons in good standing; that they were last members of the respective Lodges named opposite their several signatures hereunto; that they reside in or near the ———of———, in the county of———, Utah; that among them are a sufficient number of Brethren well qualified to open and hold a Lodge of Ancient, Free and Accepted Masons, and to discharge all its various duties in the three Degrees of Ancient Masonry, in accordance with established usage; that they have provided a safe and suitable Lodge room, and that, having the prosperity of the Craft at heart, and being desirous to use their best endeavors for the diffusion of its beneficent principles, they pray for a Dispensation empowering them to form, open and hold a regular Lodge at the———of——— , aforesaid, to be called———Lodge.

They have nominated, and respectfully recommend Bro.———, as the first Master; Bro.———, as the first Senior Warden; and Bro.———, as the first Junior Warden of the said Lodge, they being in all respects competent to perform all the duties of the several stations for which they are proposed; and, if the prayer of the petitioners be granted, they promise in all things strict obedience to the commands of the Grand Master, and undeviating conformity to the Constitution and Regulations of the Grand Lodge.

Dated——— , on the———day of———, A. D. 18—

Signature.*	Name and No. of Lodge.	State or Country.
(Sign full given name.)		

*Must be signed by at least seven known and approved Master Masons. Const. Art. XII Sec. 1.

FORM OF RECOMMENDATION OF A PETITION FOR THE INSTITUTION OF A NEW LODGE.

———Lodge, No.—, A. F. and A. M., ⎱
——————————————, A. D. 18—. ⎰

To the Most Worshipful———, Grand Master of Masons in Utah:

At a stated meeting of this Lodge, held at the date above written, the following preamble and resolution were adopted:

"WHEREAS, a petition for the issue of a Dispensation to open and form a new Lodge at———, in the county of———, has been presented to this Lodge for its recommendation; *and whereas*, it is known to this Lodge that the signers to said petition, ———in number, are all Master Masons in good standing, and that a safe and suitable Lodge room has been provided by them for their meetings: it is

"*Resolved*, That the establishment of said new Lodge is of manifest propriety, and will conduce to the good of the Fraternity, and that this Lodge recommends to the Grand Master the granting of the Dispensation prayed for in said petition."

15

A true copy from the minutes.

IN TESTIMONY WHEREOF, I have hereunto set my hand and affixed
[SEAL] the Seal of the Lodge aforesaid, at the date above written.

——— ———, *Secretary.*

FORM OF CERTIFICATE OF THE QUALIFICATIONS OF THE MASTER PROPOSED IN A PETITION FOR A NEW LODGE.

To the Most Worshipful ——— *Grand Master of Masons in Utah:*

The petition of———Brethren, residing, at the———of———, in the county of———, praying the Grand Master for a Dispensation to open and hold a new Lodge at said———, to be called———Lodge, having been presented to me; and Bro.———being recommended therein for nomination as the first Master of said proposed new Lodge, having been examined in open Lodge; now, I———Master of———Lodge, No.—, do hereby certify that said Bro.———is fully competent properly to open and close a Lodge and to confer the three Degrees of Masonry, and to deliver entire the several lectures thereunto appertaining.

Given at———, in the county of———, this———day of———, A. D. 18—.

——— ———, *Master.*

FORM OF PETITION FOR A CHARTER.

———UTAH———, A. D. 18—.

To the Most Worshipful Grand Lodge of Utah:

The undersigned respectfully represent that on the———day of———, A. D. 18—, a Dispensation was issued by the Grand Master, for the formation of a new Lodge at———, in the county of———, by the name of———Lodge; that on the ———day of———next ensuing, said Lodge was opened and organized, and has since continued successfully to work during the period named in said Dispensation, as will appear from its records, By-Laws, and returns, herewith presented; and that it is the anxious desire of the members of said Lodge that its existence be perpetuated.

They therefore pray that a Charter be granted to said Lodge, by the name of ———Lodge, with such number as the usage of the Grand Lodge may assign it; and recommend that Bro.———be named therein as Master, Bro.———, as Senior Warden; and Bro.———, as Junior Warden; promising, as heretofore, strict obedience to the commands of the Grand Master, and undeviating conformity to the Constitution and Regulations of the Grand Lodge.

GIVEN by instruction from, and on behalf of said Lodge, at———, this———day of———, A. D. 18—.

(Signature of members.*) ———

———

(Sign all given names in full.)

*Must be accompanied by the dimit of each subscriber.

FORM OF CERTIFICATE FOR REPRESENTATIVES TO THE GRAND LODGE.

————Lodge. No.—, A. F. and A. M., }
——————————————, A. D. 18—. }

To the Most Worshipful Grand Lodge of Utah:

This is to certify that Bro.————is the duly elected and installed Worshipful Master, Bro.————, the Senior Warden; and Bro.————, the Junior Warden of the above Lodge, and that as such they are entitled to represent this Lodge at the ————Annual Communication of the Most Worshipful Grand Lodge of Utah.

GIVEN under my hand and the Seal of the Lodge, on the day first
[SEAL.]   above written.

————*Secretary.*

FORM OF CREDENTIAL FOR A REPRESENTATIVE ELECTED BY A LODGE.

————Lodge, No.—, A. F. and A. M., }
——————————, A. D. 18—. }

To the Most Worshipful Grand Lodge of Utah:

This is to certify that, at a regular meeting of this Lodge, held at the date above written, it having been made known that neither the Master nor either of the Wardens thereof would be enabled to attend the Grand Lodge at its next Annual Communication, Bro.————, a member of the Lodge, was, by ballot, duly elected to serve as its Representative during said Communication.

IN TESTIMONY WHEREOF I have hereunto set my hand and have
caused the Secretary to affix the Seal of the Lodge, with his
[SEAL.]   attestation, at the date above written.

————, *Secretary.*   ————, *Master.*

FORM OF PETITION FOR THE DEGREES OF MASONRY.

————Utah————, A. D. 18—.

To the Worshipful Master, the Wardens and Members of————Lodge, No.—, A. F. & A. M.:

The undersigned respectfully represents, that, unbiased by friends and uninfluenced by mercenary motives, he freely and voluntarily offers himself as a candidate for the mysteries of Masonry; that he is prompted to solicit this privilege by a favorable opinion conceived of the institution, a desire for knowledge, and a sincere wish to be serviceable to his fellow creatures; that he has resided in Utah more than one year, next preceding the date hereof; that he has not within six months past, been rejected by any Lodge of Ancient, Free and Accepted Masons;

and that he promises, if found **worthy**, **to conform** to all the ancient usages and regulations of the Fraternity.

Residence, ————

Place of nativity, ————.

Age, ————.

Occupation, ————.   (Sign given name in full.)

Recommended by

————. } (Must be **members** of the Lodge.)

————. }

FORM OF APPLICATION FOR MEMBERSHIP.

————UTAH————, A. D. 18—.

To the Worshipful Master, Wardens and Brethren of—— Lodge, *No.*—, *A. F. & A. M.:*

The undersigned represents, that he is a Master Mason in good **standing; that** he was **last** a member of————Lodge, No.—, in the————of————, **from which he** has honorably withdrawn, **as by** the accompanying certificate will appear; **and** that he **now** desires, if found **worthy**, to become a member of your Lodge.

Residence, ————.

Age, ————.

Occupation, ————.

Place of nativity————.   ————

Lodge in which Initiated, ————.   (Sign given name in full.)

Recommended by

————, (Must be members of the Lodge.)

————,)

FORM OF CERTIFICATE OF ELECTION AND INSTALLATION OF THE OFFICERS OF A CONSTITUENT LODGE.

————LODGE, NO.—, A. F. AND A. M., (

————————, A. D. 18—.)

To the Right Worshipful Grand Secretary of the Grand Lodge of Utah:

I hereby certify that at the stated meeting of this Lodge held on the day above written, it being that **next** preceding the anniversary of St. John, the Evangelist, the following Officers were duly elected for the ensuing Masonic year, viz:

Bro.————, Master;

Bro.————, Sen. Warden;

Bro.————, Jun Warden;

Bro.————, Treasurer;

Bro ————, Secretary.

And that on the——day of——, A. D. 18—, said Officers were duly installed by (here give the name and Masonic title of the installing Officer).

GIVEN under my hand and the Seal of the Lodge, on the day first [SEAL.] above written.

——, *Secretary*

FORM OF NOTICE OF REJECTIONS, SUSPENSIONS, EXPULSIONS AND RESTORATIONS.

——LODGE No.—, A. F. AND A. M., ˧
——————————, A. D. 18— ˧

To the Right Worshipful——, Grand Secretary of the Grand Lodge of Utah:

I hereby certify that, at a regular meeting of this Lodge held at the date above written, the petition of——, an applicant for the degrees of Masonry, was rejected.

(*Or*, Bro.——, after due notice, as prescribed in the By-Laws, was suspended from all the rights and privileges of Masonry, for non-payment of dues.)

(*Or*, Bro.—— after due trial, in the manner prescribed in the Trial Code, was declared to be suspended from all the rights and privileges of Masonry, for un-Masonic conduct.)

(*Or*, Bro.——after due trial, in the manner prescribed in the Trial Code, was declared to be expelled from all the rights and privileges of Masonry, for un-Masonic conduct.)

(*Or*, Bro.——, heretofore suspended by this Lodge for non-payment of dues having paid up all arrearages (or having had his dues remitted by the Lodge), as provided in the By-Laws, resumed his rights and privileges as a Mason and as a member of this Lodge.)

(*Or*, Bro.——, heretofore suspended by this Lodge for un-Masonic conduct, was, by a two thirds vote, in the manner prescribed in the Trial Code, restored to all his rights and privileges as a Mason and as a member of this Lodge.

GIVEN under my hand and the Seal of the Lodge aforesaid, at the [SEAL.] date first above written.

——, *Secretary.*

FORM OF SUMMONS.

HALL OF——LODGE, No.—, A. F. & A. M. ˧
——————————, A. D. 18—. ˧

Mr.——Dear Sir and Brother:

You are hereby summoned to attend a——meeting of the above Lodge on ——, 18—, at——M.

Of this take due notice and govern yourself accordingly.

By order of the Worshipful Master.

——, *Secretary.*

[SEAL.]
16

FORM OF NOTICE TO ATTEND A LODGE MEETING.

HALL OF————LODGE, No.—, A. F. AND A. M.)
————————, A. D. 18—·)

Mr.————, Dear Sir and Brother

You are hereby fraternally requested to attend a————meeting of the above Lodge on-————,18—, at————M.

Yours,

[SEAL.]   ————Secretary.

———

FORM OF NOTICE FOR LODGE DUES.

HALL OF————LODGE, No.—, A. F. AND A. M.,)
————————, A. D. 18—.)

Mr.————, Dear Sir and Brother:

You are indebted to this Lodge————dollars———— cents for Dues.

I call your attention to the following Sections in the By-Laws of this Lodge, viz: (Copy sections in By-Laws referring to the payment of dues.)

The same will be strictly enforced, unless your indebtedness is promptly settled.

Of this take due notice and govern yourself accordingly.

Fraternally Yours,

[SEAL]   ————, *Secretary*

———

FORM OF· NOTICE TO A BROTHER APPOINTED ON A COMMITTEE OF INVESTI-GATION.

HALL OF————LODGE, No.—, A. F. AND A. M.,)
————————, A. D. 18—.)

Mr.————, Dear Sir and Brother:

At a regular meeting of————Lodge, No.—, A. F. and A. M., held at their Hall on the above date, you were appointed to act with Bros.————, as a Com-mittee of Investigation on the petition of Mr.————for the three Degrees in Ma-sonry (or on the petition of Bro.————for affiliation.)

His residence is————, place of nativity,————, age————, occupation, recommended by Bros.————.

Your report will be due————, 18—.

By order of the Worshipful Master,

[SEAL.]   ————, *Secretary*.

———

FORM OF DIMIT.

To all Ancient, Free and Accepted Masons wheresoever dispersed around the Globe, Greeting:

THIS IS TO CERTIFY that Brother————whose signature appears in the margin hereof, is a MASTER MASON in good standing, and was, until this date, a member

of our——Lodge, No.——, A. F. & A. M., under the jurisdiction of the M.·.
W.·. Grand Lodge of Utah. Having paid all dues, and being in good fellowship
with the Brethren, he has voluntarily withdrawn from our said Lodge; and now
by its order, receives this CERTIFICATE, recommending him to the friendship and
good will of the Fraternity wherever he may be.

GIVEN at the Hall of our Lodge aforesaid at——in the County
of——, Utah, this the——day of——A. D. 18—, as
witness my hand, the Seal of our Lodge, and the attestation of

[SEAL.]   our Secretary,   ——*Worsh. Master.*

ATTEST:——, *Secretary.*

On the back of each dimit issued in this Grand Jurisdiction shall be printed
the following:

STANDING RESOLUTION NO. 11.

[Adopted at the Third Annual Communication of the Grand Lodge of Utah, held Nov.
10th, A. D. 1874.]

Resolved, That all Non-Affiliated Masons in this Jurisdiction shall have the
privilege of visiting Lodges for the period of six months, but such Non-Affiliates
shall petition some Lodge within thirty days thereafter for membership, or contribute to some chartered Lodge in this Jurisdiction its regular dues, and in case
of non-compliance, shall be debarred from all Masonic rights and privileges, as
follows: First, They shall not be allowed to visit any Lodge. Second, They
shall not be allowed to appear in any Masonic procession. Third, They shall not
be entitled to Masonic charity. Fourth, They shall not be entitled to Masonic
burial. They shall be deemed drones in the hive of Masonry, and unworthy our
protection as Masons.

Rules & Regulations of Grand Lodge Library.

—————

RULE 1.—All Masons who are contributing members of constituent Masonic Bodies in Utah; all honorary and life members and all annual subscribers, have the privilege to visit the Library and take out books.

RULE 2.—Each book has a label on the inside cover, stating how long the book can be kept, and for each day kept over the specified time, the holder will be subject to a fine of ten cents.

RULE 3.—Masons qualified as in Rule 1, residing within this Territory, but a distance of twenty-five miles, or more, from Salt Lake City, may retain books double the length of time specified on said labels; and in such cases renewals of issuance may be made upon written application.

RULE 4.—Any Mason retaining a volume ninety days from the date of its receipt, and neglecting or refusing to pay the price of the same, or the set to which it belongs, shall be subject to Masonic discipline.

RULE 5.—The holder of a book may renew its issuance immediately after the expiration of the specified time by making application for that purpose, but under no condition will he be permitted to take it out for a third time.

RULE 6.—Every member has the privilege to take out two books at the same time, but no more.

RULE 7.—No member shall take any book from the shelves without notifying the Librarian or his representative, and having his name and the number of the book registered, and on returning the same he shall place it on the Librarian's table for his inspection, who alone shall replace books on the shelves.

RULE 8.—If a work of one volume be injured, defaced or lost, the holder must pay the value of the book. If a volume or more of a set of books be injured, defaced or lost, the full value of the whole set must be made good by the holder, who may thereupon receive the remaining volumes as his property.

RULE 9.—Members to whose name a book is charged, shall be responsible for the same.

RULE 10.—Books bearing on the label the word "Reference," cannot be taken from the Library room, and any member doing so will be fined two dollars.

RULE 11.—Any member defacing, injuring or soiling any book of reference, shall pay the full value of the volume, and in that case may claim it as his property.

RULE 12.—Any member who shall mutilate or ruin the papers placed on the files or tables in the room, or remove them therefrom, shall be fined two dollars.

RULE 13.—All fines and penalties hereby provided for, will be strictly enforced, and any member refusing to pay such fines or penalties, when notified to do so, will forfeit his privileges and lose all his rights as a member until payment is made.

RULE 14.—Children will not be permitted in the Library room, nor be allowed to take out books.

DUTIES OF A GRAND REPRESENTATIVE.

First: To visit at all regular sittings the Grand Lodge to which he is accredited, interchange published proceedings and deposit with the Grand Secretary copies of all official documents emanating from the appointing power.

Second: To acquaint himself thoroughly with the Constitution, Code of Jurisprudence and Forms of Work in vogue in the Grand Lodge which he represents, that so he may be able to communicate them, when desired, to the Grand Lodge to which he is accredited.

Third: To welcome, vouch for, and introduce worthy Masons from the jurisdiction which he represents; to detect imposters, if any, and to see to the judicious distribution of charity when demanded.

Fourth: To strengthen the golden chain of pure attachment between the Grand Lodge, encourage mutual customs and good will and give due warning of perils that may threaten to both.

17

Historical Sketch of Ancient Craft Masonry

IN THE year 1857, by order of President James Buchanan, an army of nearly three thousand men, under command of Col. Albert Sidney Johnston, was sent forward to the Territory of Utah, reaching its destination late in September. During the following winter this army camped at Fort Bridger. June 26th, 1858, it marched through this city and moved to and established Camp Floyd, fifty miles southeast of Salt Lake City. At that time Utah was not much known and almost isolated, and the mail facilities were but limited.

Among the military were a few Brothers who had been made Masons in various parts of our common country, and to practice in their solitude the teachings of Masonry, as a body, resolved to organize a Lodge. They petitioned the M∴ W∴ Samuel H. Saunders, Grand Master of Masons of Missouri, for a Dispensation, which was granted.

The following is a copy of a communication received by the writer of this sketch from the late R∴ W∴ George Frank Gouley, Grand Secretary of Missouri, in relation to this, the first regular Masonic Lodge in Utah:

"On March 6th, 1859, Bro. Anthony O'Sullivan, R∴ W∴ Grand Secretary of the M∴ W∴ Grand Lodge of Missouri, issued a Dispensation to John C. Robinson, Henry W. Tracy, C. L. Stephenson, M. S. Howe, Daniel Ruggles, W. L. Halsey, D. H. Brotherton, Benjamin Wingate and William Kearney, to open Rocky Mountain Lodge in Utah Territory, at Camp Floyd, with the following Officers: John C. Robinson, Worshipful Master; Henry W. Tracy, Senior Warden; and Carter L. Stephenson, Junior Warden."

This Dispensation was used until the succeeding session of our Grand Lodge, when a charter was issued, dated June 1st, 1860, to the above named Officers and Brethren, and said Lodge named Rocky Mountain Lodge, No. 205, to be held at Camp Floyd, Utah. The charter was signed by Marcus H. McFarland, Grand Master and attested by A. O'Sullivan, Grand Secretary.

"Among the papers I find a letter from Bro. Richard Wilson, of the 4th Artillery, the Secretay, dated March 27th, 1861, enclosing annual returns to Dec. 27th, 1860, and announcing that the name of the Post had been changed from

Camp Floyd to Fort Crittenden. The membership was composed principally of officers and soldiers of the U. S. army then quartered there, and when the location was changed to New Mexico, the charter, jewels, records, etc., were all returned to this office, more perfectly arranged, and the accounts, etc., more correctly completed than that ever received from any surrendered Lodge under the jurisdiction of this Grand Body since its organization.

"The jewels and working tools were of the very best quality, in fact every thing received by this office from that Lodge bore evidence of more than ordinary refinement and culture. The relationship between this Grand Lodge and her daughter Lodge in the then 'Great Far West,' was of a very affectionate character and the same spirit has ever been manifest between her and the former members of that Lodge."

Thus ended the first attempt of planting Masonry on Utah soil. Whether any members of this early Lodge are yet among the living, or whether one and all have marched into the celestial Lodge above, we know not. One civilian however, Bro. Nicholas S. Ransohoff, who participated in the meetings of the Lodge, although not a member, resides still in our midst, and is the only witness now here of the noble deeds of that band of true Masons composing Rocky Mountain Lodge, No. 205, at Camp Floyd, in the Territory of Utah.

In 1863, Gen. E. P. Connor arrived with two regiments of California volunteers in this city and established Camp Douglas. This attracted the attention of disappointed miners and business men in our neighboring Territory Nevada, who immigrated hither. Some of these were Masons. They considered the advisability of establishing a Lodge in this city, and for the purpose of organizing, assembled on the 11th day of November, 1865, at the Odd Fellows' Hall. Among the assembled Brethren we find the names of James M. Ellis, William G. Higley, Louis Cohn, William L. Halsey, Theodore H. Auerbach, Oliver Durant, Charles Popper and James Thurmond.

A resolution was passed to organize a Lodge, and to petition the Most Worshipful Grand Master of Nevada, for a Dispensation. James M. Ellis was nominated as the first Master, William G. Higley as Senior Warden and William L. Halsey as Junior Warden. Lander Lodge, No. 8, at Austin, Nevada, recommended the petition. The then Grand Master of Masons in Nevada, Most Worshipful Joseph DuBell responded immediately to the request and issued his letter of Dispensation for Mount Moriah Lodge, to be located at Salt Lake City, Utah. But to this Dispensation was an edict attached, requiring the Lodge to be careful, and "exclude all who were of the Mormon faith."

The first meeting of Mount Moriah Lodge was held February 5th, 1866. The two thousand volunteers in camp Douglas and the discovery of gold mines in Montana made Salt Lake City lively and business improving; and with this the Lodge prospered. Master Masons gathered around her altar and "good men and true" from the profane world petioned for the degrees. For a while perfect peace and harmony prevailed, but the above cited edict disturbed the waters from underneath and with it the rolling waves soon showed itself on the surface.

At the second Annual Communication of the Grand Lodge of Nevada, held September 18th, 1866, the Lodge petitioned for a charter. On this petition the Committee on Charters reported as follows: " * * We find the records fairly kept. In view of the peculiar circumstances surrounding the Brethren of Mt. Moriah Lodge, we would recommend that a charter be not granted at this Grand Communication, but that the Dispensation be continued for one year."

At the third Annual Communication of the Grand Lodge of Nevada, held Sept. 17th, 1867, another petition for a charter was again refused and the Dispensation discontinued. The Grand Lodge, however, instructed the Grand Secretary to issue certificates of good standing to each member of the Lodge, and donated to the Lodge its furniture and jewels. And thus ended the short career of Mount Moriah Lodge U. D. under the Grand Lodge of Nevada; but the seed it had sown in Utah had fallen on tillable soil and soon bore flowers and wholesome fruit.

In June, 1866, a Craftsman arrived in Salt Lake City to whose ability as a Masonic organizer, and to whose skill as a master builder, Freemasonry in Utah is more indebted for its present standing than to any other Mason, living or dead. Most Worshipful Reuben Howard Robertson, Past Grand Master of Utah, came here from the Territory of Montana. While in Montana, he assisted in the formation of Nevada Lodge, No. 4, and presided over it as Master. A glance at our beautiful city convinced him that she had a bright future before her; he concluded to make it his home and opened a law office in Main street. He was agreeably surprised to find here a Masonic Lodge in operation and paid it a fraternal visit. His far-seeing eye soon discoved that another Lodge could be easily built up and his noble heart and his knowledge of Masonry in all its branches soon gathered around him the sojourning Masons in this city and Camp Douglas who passed resolutions to petition the Grand Master of Montana for a Dispensation to open Wasatch Lodge.

The petition being recommended by Mt. Moriah Lodge, the Grand Master M∴ W∴ John J. Hull, of Montana, issued a Dispensation, dated October 22d, A. D. 1866, to Wasatch Lodge, to be located at Great Salt Lake City, with Bro. R. H. Robertson, as Master; Bro. Joseph Milton Orr, as Senior Warden; and Bro. Stephen DeWolfe, as Junior Warden. The following Brethren were members of the Lodge at the organization: H. S. Bohm, Treasurer; R. D. Clark, Secretary; O. F. Strickland, Senior Deacon; J. K. Sutterly, Junior Deacon; H. Ruben, Tyler; and Felix Rheinbold, Elias B. Zabriskie, Samuel Davis, Louis Engler, John Meeks, —— Gardiner, Louis Goldstein and Henry Myers. The first meeting of the Lodge was held Friday evening, November 30th, 1866.

The Lodge had an unusual success, but with such a Master as Bro. Robertson, it could not be otherwise. The so-called Webb-Preston work had been practised in Montana and Bro. Robertson had it as correct and perfect as a Master can have it. It was indeed a treat to listen when he conferred degrees and delivered the lectures. He made no strain to show any declamatory abilities, the words flowed from his lips easy and dignified, and through that he never failed to make an impression on the candidate before him and the Brethren present. (At the initiation and raising of the writer of this sketch, Bro. Robertson delivered the lectures, and I will never forget the effect left in my mind on these occasions.) If we add to this his administrative talent, his quick apprehension, fluent and ready speech coupled with a never-ceasing love for Masonry, we need not wonder at the success of Wasatch Lodge. The best of our Gentile citizens entered its portals and stood before its altar, and an interest was aroused in Masonry that enlivened, united and gave strength to the whole Gentile community. Social gatherings also were introduced and nothing was left undone to elevate Masonry and show it in its true light: an institution composed of "good men and true," whose benign influences produce a salutary effect upon their fellow men. And most of this was the work of Bro. Robertson. He certainly laid the foundation to the prosperity of Wasatch Lodge, and owing to his Masonic zeal the Lodge occupies to-day the first position in this Grand Jurisdiction.

In September 1867, Bro. Robertson started for Montana to be present at the second Annual Communication of the Grand Lodge. On his return he held in his hands a charter for Wasatch Lodge, No. 8, dated Oct. 7th, 1867. Under this charter the Lodge held its first meeting, Nov. 4th, 1867. Past Master, Bro. S. P. McCurdy, installed the following officers: Bros. R. H. Robertson, Master; Joseph Milton Orr, Senior Warden. George Bodenburg, Junior Warden; M. H. Walker, Treasurer and John Cunnington, Secretary. Bro. Robertson was re-elected Master in 1868 and again in 1870.

Up to spring 1867 Mount Moriah and Wasatch Lodges and Utah Lodge, No. 1, I. O. O. F., met jointly in the upper part of a building on East Temple street, known as Odd Fellows' Hall. (At present the building is occupied by the mercantile firm of Day & Co.) The hall was anything but inviting; it was small and the ceiling not over nine feet high. It was not suitable for the purposes, and arrangements were inaugurated for new and more elegant apartments, which were found in a stone building on the east side of East Temple street, on the same lot where the Masonic Hall now stands. The three Lodges moved into their new Hall in the summer, 1867. In this Hall they remained till Feb. 5th, 1872, when the Masons separated from the Odd Fellows and rented a Hall by themselves in Trowbridge's building, where they met till November, 1876. The present Masonic Hall, on the third floor of the first National Bank building, was dedicated for Masonic purposes by M.˙. W.˙. Edmund P. Johnson, assisted by the Grand Lodge of Utah, Nov. 14th, 1876.

We must now turn upon another page of Mt. Moriah Lodge. We stated before that the Brethren had received certificates of good standing in Masonry from the Grand Lodge of Nevada. But these dimits did not satisfy them, they were firm in their resolution to keep united as a Lodge. A petition for a Dispensation to the Grand Master of Montana was refused. Another and successful attempt was made with M.˙. W.˙. M. S. Adams, Grand Master of Kansas, who, on the 25th day of Nov., 1867, granted a Dispensation to open Mt. Moriah Lodge in this city. Under this Dispensation the Lodge held its first meeting, Dec.

18

18th, 1867. The following Brethren were the first Officers: Joseph F. Noanan, Master; William G. Higley, Senior Warden; Theodore H. Auerbach, Junior Warden; Sol. Siegel, Treasurer; Edmund P. Johnson, Secretary; Louis Cohn, Senior Deacon; Geo. B. Moulton, Junior Deacon; N. Boukofsky and Paul Engelbrecht, Stewards.

It cannot be said that Mt. Moriah Lodge made a mark while working under this Dispensation, yet it did the necessary work, and the members, having the struggle with Nevada fresh in their memories, raised among themselves a sufficient sum of money to send a delegate to Leavenworth, Kansas, with a petition for a charter. The delegate, M∴ W∴ E. P. Johnson, Past Grand Master of Utah, had by no means an easy work, the Masonic writers and reviewers throughout the land had disapproved the issuance of the Dispensation, but Bro. Johnson fought bravely for the rights of his Brethren, and a charter to Mt. Moriah Lodge, No. 70, was granted at Leavenworth, Kansas, October 21st, 1868.

November 9th, 1868, the Lodge held its first meeting under this charter. Bro. Robertson installed the Officers, they being the same as they were U. D. with the exception of Bro. Sol. Siegel, who was installed as Secretary, and Bro. Elias Ransohoff, as Treasurer. The undersigned having been initiated in this Lodge, Sept. 2d, 1868, being passed therein Nov. 9th, 1868, and raised Dec. 9th, 1868, and who has occupied for five consecutive years the offices of Secretary, for one year of Senior Warden and for two years of Master, and is still a member thereof must leave it to a future chronicler to say whether Mt. Moriah Lodge has filled her mission in the Body Masonic or whether she has neglected to do her share of Masonic deeds.

In 1870, a change for the better took place in Utah. The great Pacific railroad had laid its last rail in Oct. 1869, near Promontory Point, and Utah was in daily communication with the large and populous cities on the Atlantic and Pacific oceans. We were no longer isolated. With the blowing of the steam whistle through Echo and Weber Canyons, civilization had found its way into Utah, and with it came a large Gentile immigration, making Salt Lake City its rallying point. Miners prospected the Wasatch and Oquirrh mountains, and with drill and pick opened their hidden treasures; capitalists erected smelters and refining works and merchants new warehouses; all of which gave new life, vigor and hopes to the old residents. The cloud that for many years overshadowed our adopted home had burst; the sky was clear and promised a bright future.

Our neighboring States, Nevada and California, furnished a valuable share of the new immigration, and Masonry having taken deep root in both of these States a fresh activity soon showed itself in our city Lodges, and the formation of a third Lodge was talked of, the main point of which was to establish at an early day a Grand Lodge of Ancient, Free and Accepted Masons of Utah, and with it frustrate the notions of some men, high in power, to obtain Dispensations and Charters for Masonic Lodges in Utah, from foreign countries.

The Grand Master of Masons of Colorado, Henry M. Teller, was in 1871 in this city, and he being advised in the matter promised a Dispensation for a new

Lodge, if the proper application would be made. This being done, Grand Master Teller issued a letter of Dispensation, dated at the Grand East of Colorado, April 8th, A. D. 1871, authorizing the following Brethren to open Argenta Lodge U. D. at Salt Lake City: Ebenezer H. Shaw, Master; Elias B. Zabriskie, Senior Warden; Martin K. Harkness, Junior Warden; Edward Reed, Treasurer; A. S. Gould, Secretary; L. B. Thurman, Senior Deacon; Samuel Woodward, Junior Deacon; and Thomas A. Bates, Warren Hussey, W. S. Woodhull and F. D. McKenna. Under this Dispensation Argenta Lodge held its first meeting May 9th, 1871.

At the eleventh Annual Communication of the Grand Lodge of Colorado a petition was received from Argenta Lodge for a charter. The petition was granted and the charter to Argenta Lodge, No. 21, issued on the 26th day of September, 1871. At the first meeting of the Lodge under this charter, held Nov. 7th, 1871, Bro. Reuben H. Robertson installed the following elected Officers: Ebenezer H. Shaw, Master (died in England, February 10th, 1876); Elias B. Zabriskie, Senior Warden; A. W. Nuckolls, Junior Warden; Theodore F. Tracy, Treasurer; and A. S. Gould, Secretary. The Lodge at that time had fourteen members, among them we notice the names of Bros. L. B. Thurman, Charles K. Gilchrist, J. M. Haskill, Charles D. Handy, H. Armer and Levant Peace.

Argenta Lodge, No. 21, since its organization, has done true work and square work; before its altar many good men have been obligated and initiated into the mystic Brotherhood, and many of its members have occupied and filled creditably elevated stations in our Grand Lodge, and that others from its ranks will be elected to govern the Craft in Utah, none will doubt.

The third Lodge was now established and the foundation for the main edifice could be laid. Wasatch, Mount Moriah and Argenta Lodges agreed, in the first and last named, unanimously, in Mount Moriah with a large majority, to establish a Grand Lodge. The preliminary arrangements were soon made, and on the 16th day of January, 1872, at 2 o'clock P. M., the following Masters and Wardens of the three Lodges met in their Hall, for the purpose of organizing the Grand Lodge of Utah: Bros. J. M. Orr, M. H. Walker and Morris Meyer, from Wasatch Lodge, No. 8; Louis Cohn, Sol Siegel and Charles F. Smith, from Mt. Moriah Lodge, No. 70; A. S. Gould, proxy for E. H. Shaw, W∴ M∴, E. B. Zabriskie and A. W. Nuckolls, from Argenta Lodge, No 21. Bro. J. M. Orr was elected Chairman of the convention and Bro. A. S. Gould, Secretary. Bro. Louis Cohn offered the necessary resolution for the formation and organization of the Grand Lodge of Utah, which was unanimously carried. The charters of the three Lodges were examined and having been found correct, an election of Grand Officers was held resulting as follows: Bros. O. F. Strickland, Grand Master; Louis Cohn, Deputy Grand Master; E. B. Zabriskie, Senior Grand Warden; A. S. Gould, Junior Grand Warden; Charles F. Smith, Grand Treasurer; and Jos. F. Nounnan, Grand Secretary. Bro. Nounnan requested the Grand Master to appoint the undersigned, as Assistant Grand Secretary, who was summoned at his place of business to appear in Grand Lodge without delay for installation.

The elected and appointed Grand Officers were installed by Bro. Reuben H. Robertson, a Constitution and code of By-Laws adopted, the three Lodges directed to return their charters to the respective Grand Lodges, receiving therefor new charters from the Grand Lodge of Utah, with numbers according to the date of their old charters. Wasatch being the oldest chartered Lodge received number 1, Mt. Moriah, number 2 and Argenta. number 3. At the organization of the Grand Lodge, Wasatch Lodge had forty-eight members on its roll, Mt. Moriah fifty-two and Argenta twenty-four, total one hundred and twenty-four Master Masons in the Grand Jurisdiction of Utah.

None of the Lodges were over-burdened with funds and a large increase of members was, under the circumstances, not probable. Let no one think that the founders of the Grand Lodge considered its maintenance an easy work and light task; on the contrary, every Brother knew the importance of the step that had been taken and a close observer could read in every eye that the grave responsibilities resting upon them were deeply felt. At this moment of despondency Bro. Robertson arose and delivered, before the final adjournment, a short address to the assembled Brethren, closing with: " Now we launch our little craft upon the great Masonic sea. We doubt not but in the future, as in the past, storms will arise, the wind will howl and whistle above, and the troubled waters roll beneath us, but with a steady hand at the helm, with the Bible as our Polar Star, the compass as our guide, and 'Brotherly Love, Relief and Truth,' as our motto, we can wrestle with the contending waves and ride upon their billows. We need never cast anchor for repairs."

During the delivery of the address, which was wholly without preparation, not a breath could be heard in the Hall, but at the conclusion, all went to their feet, joy beamed in every eye, one grasped the others hand, and with a firm resolution to succeed in the undertaking parted in peace and harmony.

Bro. Robertson is no more. On the 4th day of January, 1879, he entered into the Grand Lodge, presided over by the G∴ A∴ O∴ T∴ U∴, but he had the satisfaction of seeing the Grand Lodge of Utah recognized by every Grand Lodge on the globe, occupying an enviable position among her sisters, and that his encouraging and prophetic words, spoken on that memorable 20th of January, 1872, had been fulfilled. Up to this day, the Grand Lodge of Utah has had no need "to cast anchor for repairs."

Grand Master Strickland being Judge of the first U. S. District Court, with its seat at Provo, Utah County, and Bro. Ira M. Swartz, the clerk of the court, both zealous Masons, worked energetically for a Lodge at their home, to be called Utah Lodge. A petition for its formation was granted on the 15th of February, 1872, and the Lodge commenced work on the 16th of February, with the following Officers and members : Bros. Ira M. Swartz, Master; Charles S. Benham, Senior Warden; Samuel Paul, Junior Warden; Benjamin Bachman, Secretary, and F. H. Simmons, John P. Doolan, Samuel E. Greeley, Still P. Taft and John N. Whitney.

The Master of Utah Lodge, Bro. Swartz, was a well-skilled Mason and labored faithfully for the success of the Lodge. At the first Annual Communication of the Grand Lodge a petition from the Lodge for a charter was received and granted under the name of Story Lodge, No. 4, to be located at Provo, the charter bearing date October 8th, 1872. The Lodge selected the name of "Story" in memory of a dear friend of Bro. Swartz, Bro. W. R. Story, a former member of Wasatch Lodge, who was assassinated in the discharge of his duties as a U. S. officer, near Tooele, in 1870.

The Grand Lodge held its first Annual Communication, on the 7th of October, 1872, at which Bros. R. A. Robertson was elected Grand Master, Louis Cohn, Deputy Grand Master; J. M. Orr, Senior Grand Warden; A. W. Nuckolls, Junior Grand Warden; Charles F. Smith, Grand Treasurer; and Christopher Diehl, Grand Secretary. At this Communication, it was discovered that the Laws adopted at the organization were very defective, and a committee was appointed to revise the Code, and in order to give it sufficient time to perfect its work, the Grand Lodge was called from labor for the space of thirty days. The Grand Lodge re-assembled Nov. 12th, and the Committee on the revision of the Code reported. The present Constitution, Laws and Regulations, as prepared by the Committee, were adopted and since then have been but slightly changed or amended.

On the 15th of October, 1872, Grand Master Robertson issued a letter of Dispensation to Corinne Lodge U. D., located at Corinne, Box Elder County, naming therein Bros. E. P. Johnson as Master, Louis Demars as Senior Warden, and James A. Farnum as Junior Warden. By virtue of this Dispensation the Lodge held its first meeting on the following day, Oct. 16th, and from that day up to October 15th, 1873, the Lodge had received thirty-eight applications for the three Degrees. Of these seventeen were rejected, twenty candidates were initiated, twenty passed and nineteen raised. The petition of the Lodge for a charter was granted Nov. 11th, 1873, and on the 25th of November, Grand Master Louis Cohn, accompanied by the principal Officers of the Grand Lodge, instituted Corinne Lodge, No. 5.

On St. John's Day, Dec. 27th, 1873, Grand Master Louis Cohn granted a Dispensation to Weber Lodge U. D., located at Ogden, Weber County, with Bros. C. S. Nellis as Master, A. D. Shakespeare as Senior Warden, and Henry Bruce as Junior Warden. This Lodge received a charter from the Grand Lodge, Nov. 12th, 1874, and was instituted by Grand Master, Charles W. Bennett, accompanied by several other Grand Officers, Nov. 17th, 1874.

It is not the intention of this sketch to enumerate every transaction of the Grand Lodge of Utah since its organization, neither those of its constituent Lodges. The annual printed proceedings of the Grand Lodge give all the necessary information of its actions, rise and progress in the good work of Masonry. To these Proceedings the searcher for a more detailed history is referred. This sketch is only designed to give a short synopsis of the early struggles of Masonry in Utah, and if this has been done in the foregoing pages, to the understanding and satisfaction of the Craft in Utah, the task is accomplished.

19

There is, however, one institution connected with Masonry and the Grand Lodge of Utah, which requires, before concluding this sketch, a few lines, as it is, from the present outlook designed to occupy in the future a prominent niche, not only in the history of Masonry but also of the Gentile community in Utah, namely: The Grand Lodge Library. Originally the Library was intended for Masonic publications only, to which the Grand Librarian added books relating to the history of the Territory of Utah and Mormonism. The Grand Lodge appropriated liberally to the support of this storehouse of knowledge, and two years after its establishment, in November, 1874, there were on the shelves one hundred and seventy-nine volumes.

Grand Master, Charles W. Bennett, devoted in his address, in 1875, the following sentiments to the Library:

"At present most of our books treat of Masonic subjects, and it would be hard to find a more complete collection. An extension of the plan will soon make the Library embrace books of science and general literature with history, biography and the like. If you will take the scheme to your good Masonic hearts, and fasten it, I can foresee that the time will speedily come when Brethren who may be among us, far from the sacred influences of happy homes, seeking fortunes in our Rocky Mountain treasure vaults, and our own young men who are liable to the thousand temptations of the frontier life, may be shielded from evil by the kindly influences which our Library of the future may offer them. But should you think this, my vision, too highly tinted with the rosy hue, you will agree that every Mason should industriously store his mind with useful knowledge, and that so far as we can, we should encourage all to do so, and render all the aid in our power to that end."

These sentiments of Bro. Bennett were the opinion of the Grand Librarian at the founding of the Library and their echo produced the greatest happiness in his heart and mind. But owing to the limited room at the Masonic Hall the suggestion of Bro. Bennett, though well received and approved by the Grand Lodge, could not be carried into effect. The five Masonic Bodies at Salt Lake City, in renting their present Hall secured with it a large room on the second floor of the building, designing it for a Library and reading-room.

With this addition the Library project received a new impetus. The former Ladies' Library Association donated, under certain conditions, for our use over nine hundred volumes, and a Committee appointed by the Grand Lodge, consisting of Bros. Charles W. Bennett, Frank Tilford and Samuel Kahn, collected in aid of the Library from citizens of this city the large sum of twenty-five hundred dollars. New books were immediately purchased, and on the 1st of September, 1877, the Library was opened for the use and benefit of the Craft and general public, and kept open two hours every day. At that time the Library contained seventeen hundred and eighty-six books of a general character and three hundred and sixty of a Masonic character. The Library soon became the pride of every Utah Mason, and to the honor of Wasatch, Mt. Moriah and Argenta Lodges and Utah Chapter and Commandery be it here recorded, that each contributed nobly toward its maintenance. These five Bodies have done, and do all they can to support the Library, and without their monthly contributions it could not exist.

The readers and patrons of the Library increased steadily, and to extend its usefulness it became a necessity to keep it open from 10 o'clock A. M. to 9 o'clock P. M., which commenced Dec. 1st 1877. In November, 1878, the Library contained twenty-four hundred and sixty volumes, embracing every branch of general literature and four hundred and nineteen volumes on Masonry. To-day the Masonic Library is considered to be one of the best public institutions of Salt Lake City. It has done its share of good in the past; it will do more in the future. The constant aim of the Craft in Utah should be the progress of the Library; with it we demonstrate the intellectual advancement of mankind, the standard bearers of which ought to be the Freemasons wheresoever dispersed, because they have been in times past, and forever will be, searchers for "more Light."

CHRISTOPHER DIEHL.

SALT LAKE CITY, April 1st, 1879.

* 9 7 8 3 3 3 7 2 1 9 7 0 3 *